12 + 1 SAMPLE PAPERS

KAUSHLESH DWIVEDI

EDUCATOR

M.Sc. (Chemistry), B.Ed. (Science)

Board sample paper with solution & analysis based on latest circular issue in July for 2022-23 exam.

Title : ICSE Class 10 Biology

Author Name : Mr. Kaushlesh Dwivedi

Published By : EduGorilla Community Pvt. Ltd.

Publishers Address : Sector-12/651, First Floor Opp. Arvindo Park,
Near Jama Masjid, Indira Nagar, Lucknow,
Uttar Pradesh-226016, India

Copyright

ISBN: 9789355564917

+91-63932 16806, +91-78000 04200
book@edugorilla.com
www.edugorilla.com

Disclaimer

Created & Compiled by EduGorilla Publication

Printed by EduGorilla Community Pvt. Ltd.

INDEX

CBSE X BIOLOGY

TO GET FREE ACCESS SCAN THE QR CODE

* PREVIOUS YEAR PAPERS
* TOPPERS ANSWER SHEET
* STUDY NOTES & VIDEO LECTURES
* VIDEO SOLUTION OF SELF-ASSESSMENT PAPERS
* LIVE DISCUSSION ON MEQ (MOST EXPECTED QUESTIONS)

SCIENCE (52)
BIOLOGY
SCIENCE Paper - 3
CLASS X

There will be **one** written paper of **two hours** duration of **80 marks** and Internal Assessment of practical work carrying **20 marks**.

1. **Biology**

(i) Cell Cycle and Cell Division.

Cell cycle – Interphase (G_1, S, G_2) and Mitotic phase.

Cell Division:

- Mitosis and its stages.
- A basic understanding of Meiosis as a reduction division (stages not required).
- A brief idea of homologous chromosomes and crossing over leading to variations.
- Significance and major differences between mitotic and meiotic division.

(ii) Structure of chromosome.

Basic structure of chromosome with elementary understanding of terms such as chromatin, chromatid, gene structure of DNA and centromere.

(iii) Genetics: Mendel's laws of inheritance and sex-linked inheritance of diseases.

- The three laws of Mendel.
- Monohybrid cross – phenotype and genotype.
- Dihybrid cross – Only phenotype.
- The following terms to be covered: gene, allele, heterozygous, homozygous, dominant, recessive, mutation, variation, phenotype, genotype.
- Sex determination in human beings.

Sex linked inheritance of diseases to include only X-linked like haemophilia and colour blindness.

2. **Plant Physiology**

(i) Absorption by roots, imbibition, diffusion and osmosis; osmotic pressure, root pressure; turgidity and flaccidity; plasmolysis and deplasmolysis; the absorption of water and minerals; active and passive transport (in brief); The rise of water up to the xylem; Forces responsible for ascent of sap.

- Understanding of the processes related to absorption of water by the roots.
- Characteristics of roots, which make them suitable for absorbing water.
- Structure of a single full-grown root hair.
- A general idea of Cohesive, Adhesive forces and transpirational pull.
- Experiments to show the conduction of water through the xylem.

(ii) Transpiration - process and significance. Ganong's potometer and its limitations. The factors affecting rate of transpiration. Experiments on transpiration. A brief idea of guttation and bleeding.

- Concept of transpiration and its importance to plants
- Experiments related to transpiration:

(a) Loss in weight of a potted plant or a leafy shoot in a test tube as a result of transpiration.

(b) Use of cobalt chloride paper to demonstrate unequal rate of transpiration in a dorsiventral leaf.

- Adaptations in plants to reduce transpiration.
- A brief idea of guttation and bleeding.
- Photosynthesis: the process and its importance to life in general; experiments to show the necessity of light, carbon dioxide, chlorophyll, formation of starch and release of oxygen

movements in plants with reference to – Phototropism, Geotropism, Hydrotropism, Thigmotropism and Chemotropism (supported with suitable examples).

3. **Human Anatomy and Physiology**

- The process and significance of Photosynthesis.
- The internal structure of chloroplast to be explained to give an idea of the site of light and dark reactions.
- Opening and closing of stomata based on potassium ion exchange theory.
- Overall balanced chemical equation to represent photosynthesis.
- Introduction of the terms "photochemical" for light phase and "biosynthetic" for dark phases.
- Light reaction - activation of chlorophyll followed by photolysis of water, release of O_2, formation of ATP (photophosphorylation) and NADPH.
- Dark reaction - only combination of hydrogen released by NADP with CO_2 to form glucose. (detailed equations are not required).
- Adaptations in plants for photosynthesis.
- Experiments with regard to the factors essential for photosynthesis; emphasis on destarching and the steps involved in starch test.

(iv) Chemical coordination in Plants: A general study of plant growth regulators; Tropic movements in plants.

- A brief idea of the physiological effects of Auxins, Gibberellins, Cytokinins, Abscisic acid and Ethylene in regulating the growth of plants.
- the main blood vessels entering and leaving the heart, liver and kidney will be required). Lymphatic system.

(i) Circulatory System: Blood and lymph, the structure and working of the heart, blood vessels, circulation of blood (only names of

- A basic understanding of the tropic
- Brief idea of tissue fluid and lymph.
- Increase in efficiency of mammalian red blood cells due to absence of certain organelles; reasons for the same.
- A brief idea of blood coagulation.
- Structure and working of the heart along with names of the main blood vessels entering and leaving the heart, the liver and the kidney.

- Concept of systole and diastole; concept of double circulation.
- Brief idea of pulse and blood pressure.
- the blood vessels entering and leaving the kidney; functions of various parts of the urinary system (emphasis on diagram with correct labelling). A general idea of the structure of a kidney tubule/ nephron.
- A brief idea of ultra-filtration (emphasis on the diagram of malpighian capsule); selective reabsorption and tubular secretion in relation to the composition of blood plasma and urine formed.
- Blood vessels: artery, vein and capillary to be explained with the help of diagrams to bring out the relationship between their structure and function.
- Brief idea of the lymphatic organs: spleen and tonsils.
- ABO blood group system, Rh factor.
- Significance of the hepatic portal system.

(ii) Excretory System: A brief introduction to the excretory organs; parts of the urinary system; structure and function of the kidneys; blood vessels associated with kidneys; structure and function of nephron

- A brief idea of different excretory organs in the human body.
- External and internal structure of the kidney;
- Parts of the urinary system along with

(iii)Nervous system: Structure of Neuron; central, autonomous and peripheral nervous system (in brief); brain and spinal cord; reflex action and how it differs from voluntary action.

Sense organs – Eye: Structure, functions, defects and corrective measures: Ear: Parts and functions of the ear.

- Parts of a neuron.
- Various parts of the external structure of the brain and its primary parts: Medulla Oblongata, Cerebrum, Cerebellum, Thalamus, Hypothalamus and Pons; their functions.
- Reference to the distribution of white and gray matter in Brain and Spinal cord.
- Voluntary and involuntary actions – meaning with examples.
- Diagrammatic explanation of the reflex arc, showing the pathway from receptor to effector.
- A brief idea of the peripheral and autonomic nervous system in regulating body activities.
- Differences between natural and acquired reflex.
- External and Internal structure and functions of the Eye and Ear and their various parts.
- A brief idea of stereoscopic vision, adaptation and accommodation of eye.
- Defects of the eye (myopia, hyperopia hypermetropia, presbyopia, astigmatism and cataract) and corrective measures (diagrams included for myopia and hyperopia only)
- The course of perception of sound in human ear.
- Role of ear in maintaining balance of the body.

(iv) Endocrine System: General study of the following glands: Adrenal, Pancreas, Thyroid and Pituitary. Endocrine and Exocrine glands.

- Differences between Endocrine and Exocrine glands.
- Exact location and shape of the endocrine glands in the human body.
- Hormones secreted by the following glands: Pancreas: insulin and glucagon; Thyroid: only thyroxin; Adrenal gland: Cortical hormones and adrenaline; Pituitary: growth hormone, tropic hormones, ADH and oxytocin.
- Effects of hypo secretion and hyper secretion of hormones.

(v) The Reproductive System: Organs, fertilisation functions of placenta in the growth of the embryo Menstrual cycle.

- Functions of Male and Female reproductive organs and male accessory glands. An idea of secondary sexual characters.
- Structure and functions of the various parts of the sperm and egg.
- Explanation of the terms: Fertilization, implantation, placenta, gestation and parturition.
- A brief idea of the role of placenta in nutrition, respiration and excretion of the embryo; its endocrinal function.
- Functions of Foetal membranes and amniotic fluid.
- Menstrual cycle outline of menstrual cycle.
- Role of Sex hormones: Testosterone, Oestrogen and Progesterone in reproduction.
- Identical and fraternal twins: meaning and differences only.

4. Population

Population explosion in India; need for adopting control measures - population control.

- Main reasons for the sharp rise in human population in India and in the world.
- A brief explanation of the terms: demography, population density, birth rate, death rate and growth rate of population.
- Problems faced due to population explosion: unemployment, over exploitation of natural resources, low per capita income, price rise, pollution, unequal distribution of wealth.
- Methods of population control: Surgical methods – Tubectomy and vasectomy.

5. Pollution

(i) Types and sources of pollution; major pollutants.

- Air: Vehicular, industrial, burning garbage, brick kilns.
- Water: Household detergents, sewage, industrial waste, oil spills.
- Thermal pollution.
- Soil: Industrial waste, urban commercial and domestic waste, chemical fertilizers.
- Biomedical waste – used and discarded needles, syringes, soiled dressings etc.
- Radiation: X-rays; radioactive fallout from nuclear plants.
- Noise: Motor Vehicles, Industrial establishments, Construction Sites, Loudspeakers etc.

(ii) Biodegradable and Non-biodegradable wastes

Biodegradable wastes: meaning and example; paper, vegetable peels, etc.
Non-biodegradable wastes: meaning and example; plastics, glass, Styrofoam etc. Pesticides like DDT etc.

(iii) Effects of pollution on climate, environment, human health and other organisms; control measures.

- Brief explanation of: Greenhouse effect and Global warming, Acid rain, Ozone layer depletion.
- Measures to control pollution:
  - Use of unleaded petrol / CNG in automobiles
  - Switching of engines at traffic signal lights
  - Social forestry
  - Setting of sewage treatment plants
  - Ban on polythene and plastics
  - Organic farming
  - Euro Bharat vehicular standard.

  (A brief idea of the above measures)
- A brief mention of "Swachh Bharat Abhiyan"- A national campaign for Clean India.

INTERNAL ASSESSMENT OF
PRACTICAL WORK

The practical work is designed to test the ability of the candidates to make an accurate observation from specimens of plants and animals.

PLANT LIFE

(i) Observation of permanent slides of stages of mitosis.

(ii) Experiments demonstrating:

- Diffusion: using potassium permanganate in water.
- Osmosis: Thistle Funnel experiment and potato osmoscope.
- Absorption: using a small herbaceous plant.

(iii) Experiments on Transpiration:

- demonstration of the process using a Bell Jar.
- demonstration of unequal transpiration in a dorsiventral leaf using cobalt chloride paper.
- demonstration of uptake of water and the rate of transpiration using Ganong's potometer.

(iv) Experiments on Photosynthesis:

- to show the necessity of light, carbon dioxide and chlorophyll–for photosynthesis.
- to show the release of O_2 during photosynthesis using hydrilla / elodea.

ANIMAL LIFE

(i) Identification of the structures of the urinary system, heart and kidney (internal structure) and brain (external view) through models and charts

(ii) The identification of different types of blood cells under a microscope.

(iii) Identification of the internal structure of the Ear and Eye (Through models and charts).

(iv) Identification and location of selected endocrine glands: Adrenal, Pancreas, Thyroid and Pituitary glands with the help of a models or chart.

EVALUATION

The practical work/project work are to be evaluated by the subject teacher and by an External Examiner

(The External Examiner may be a teacher nominated by the Head of the school, who could be from the faculty, **but not teaching the**

subject in the relevant section/class. For example, a teacher of Biology of Class VIII may be deputed to be an External Examiner for Class X, Biology projects.)

The Internal Examiner and the External Examiner will assess the practical work/project work independently.

Award of marks	**(20 Marks)**
Subject Teacher (Internal Examiner)	**10 marks**
External Examiner	**10 marks**

The total marks obtained out of 20 are to be sent to the Council by the Head of the school.

The Head of the school will be responsible for the online entry of marks on the Council's CAREERS portal by the due date.

INTERNAL ASSESSMENT IN SCIENCE - GUIDELINES FOR MARKING WITH GRADES

Criteria	Preparation	Procedure/ Testing	Observation	Inference/ Results	Presentation
Grade I (4 marks)	Follows instructions (written, oral, diagrammatic) with understanding; modifies if needed. Familiarity with and safe use of apparatus, materials, techniques.	Analyses problem systematically. Recognises a number of variables and attempts to control them to build a logical plan of investigation.	Records data/observations without being given a format. Comments upon, recognises use of instruments, degree of accuracy. Recording is systematic.	Processes data without format. Recognises and comments upon sources of error. Can deal with unexpected results, suggesting modifications.	Presentation is accurate and good. Appropriate techniques are well used.
Grade II (3 marks)	Follows instructions to perform experiment with step-by-step operations. Awareness of safety. Familiarity with apparatus, materials and techniques.	Specifies sequence of operation; gives reasons for any change in procedure. Can deal with two variables, controlling one.	Makes relevant observations. No assistance is needed for recording format that is appropriate.	Processes data appropriately as per a given format. Draws qualitative conclusions consistent with required results.	Presentation is adequate. Appropriate techniques are used.
Grade III (2 marks)	Follows instructions to perform a single operation at a time. Safety awareness. Familiarity with apparatus & materials.	Develops simple experimental strategy. Trial and error modifications made to proceed with the experiment.	Detailed instructions needed to record observations. Format required to record results.	Processes data approximately with a detailed format provided. Draws observations qualitative conclusions as required.	Presentation is reasonable, but disorganised in some places. Overwriting; rough work is untidy.
Grade IV (1 mark)	Follows some instructions to perform a single	Struggles through the experiment.	Format required to record	Even when detailed format is provided,	Presentation is poor and disorganised

	practical operation. Casual about safety. Manages to use apparatus & materials.	Follows very obvious experimental strategy.	observations/ readings but tends to make mistakes in recording.	struggles or makes errors while processing data. Reaches conclusions with help.	but follows an acceptable sequence. Rough work missing or untidy.
Grade V (0 marks)	Not able to follow instructions or proceed with practical work without full assistance. Unaware of safety.	Cannot proceed with the experiment without help from time to time.	Even when format is given, recording is faulty or irrelevant.	Cannot process results, nor draw conclusions, even with considerable help.	Presentation unacceptable; disorganised, untidy/ poor. Rough work missing.

Mind Map : Cell Cycle, Cell Division and Structure

Cell Cycle, Cell Division and Structure of Chromosomes

Cell Division

- Mitosis (One parent cell divides into 2 identical daughter cells)
  - Significance
    - Growth
    - Repair
    - Replacement
    - Asexual
    - Maintains same chromosome number.
  - Comprises
    - Karyokinesis (Division of nucleus)
      - Prophase: Chromosomes become visible as fine, long threads.
      - Metaphase: Chromosomes become arranged in horizontal plane at equator.
      - Anaphase: Daughter chromosomes moves to opposite poles of spindle
      - Telophase: Chromosomes lose their distinctiveness & gradually become transformed into chromatin network.
    - Cytokinesis (Division of cytoplasm)
- Meiosis (Occurs in sex cells & results in formation of four daughter cells)
  - Crossing over
  - Gamete formation
  - Reduction of Chromosome number
  - Sexual significance
  - Recombination of traits
  - Meiosis-I: Numbers of chromosomes reduced to half.
  - Meiosis-II: It is simple mitotic type.

Chromosomes

- Rod shaped or thread like deeply stained condensed chromatin fibres.
  - Types
    - Telocentric
    - Acrocentric
    - Sub-metacentric
    - Metacentric

Chromatin

- Continuous linear dsDNA associated with proteins.
- Occurs in non-dividing nucleus as chromatin fibers

DNA

- Double helical model of DNA was given by Watson & Crick
  - Consists
    - Phosphate
    - Sugar
    - Nitrogenous base
      - Adenine
      - Guanine
      - Cytosine
      - Thymine

Cell Cycle : Divide, Grow & Redivide

- Interphase
  - First growth phase- G1
  - Synthesis phase- S
  - Second growth phase -G2
- M- Phase or Mitosis

Difference between Mitosis & Meiosis

- Mitosis
  - (a) Mitosis takes place in the somatic cells.
  - (b) It is a single division which produces two cells.
  - (c) The number of chromosomes remains the same after mitosis.
  - (d) No crossing over takes place.
- Meiosis
  - (a) It occurs either in the reproductive cells or at the time of development of zygote.
  - (b) It is double division. It gives rise to four cells.
  - (c) The number of chromosomes reduced to half after meiosis.
  - (d) Crossing over takes place in prophase-I.

Trace the Mind Map
- First Level
- Second Level
- Third Level

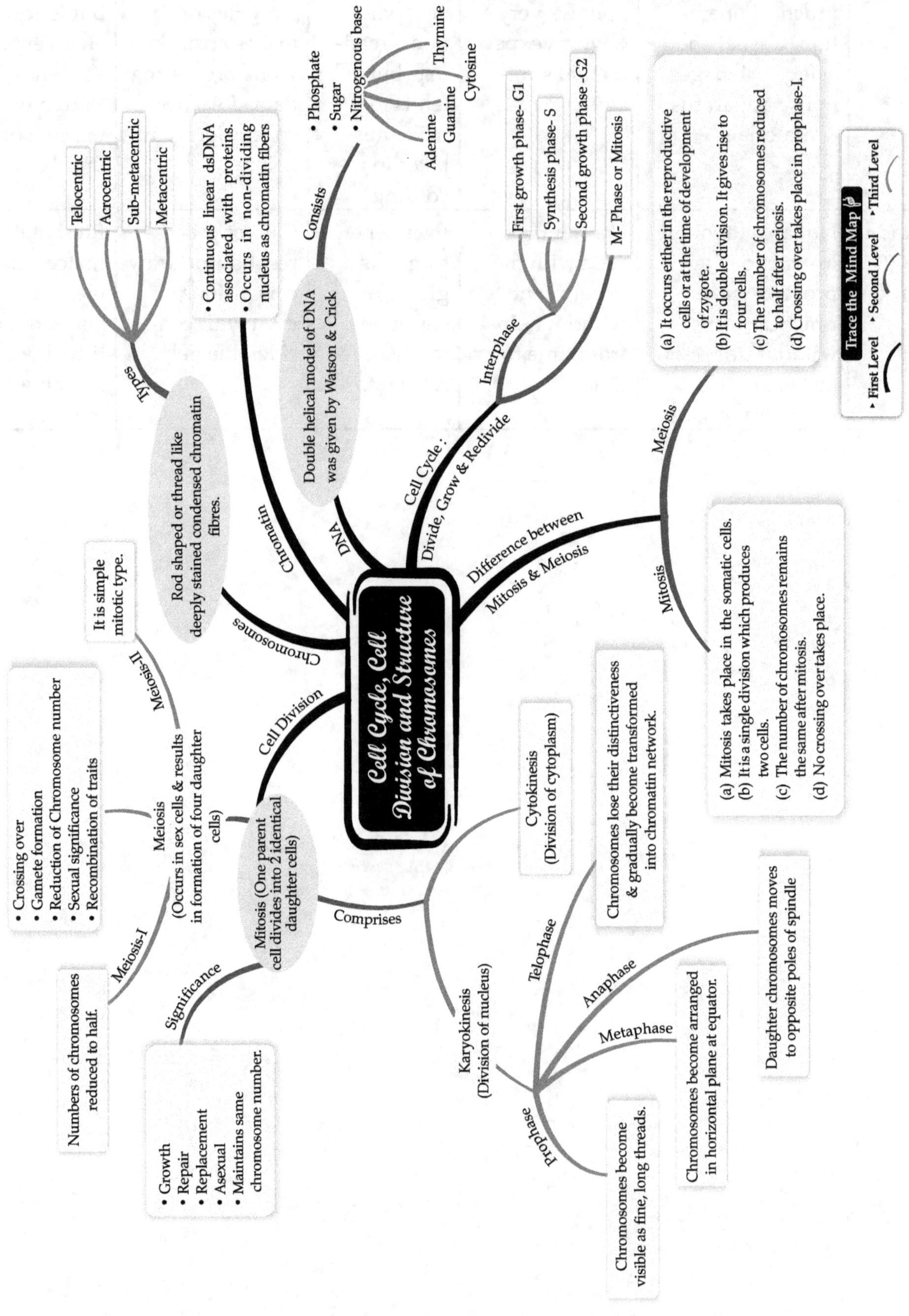

Mind Map : Genetics

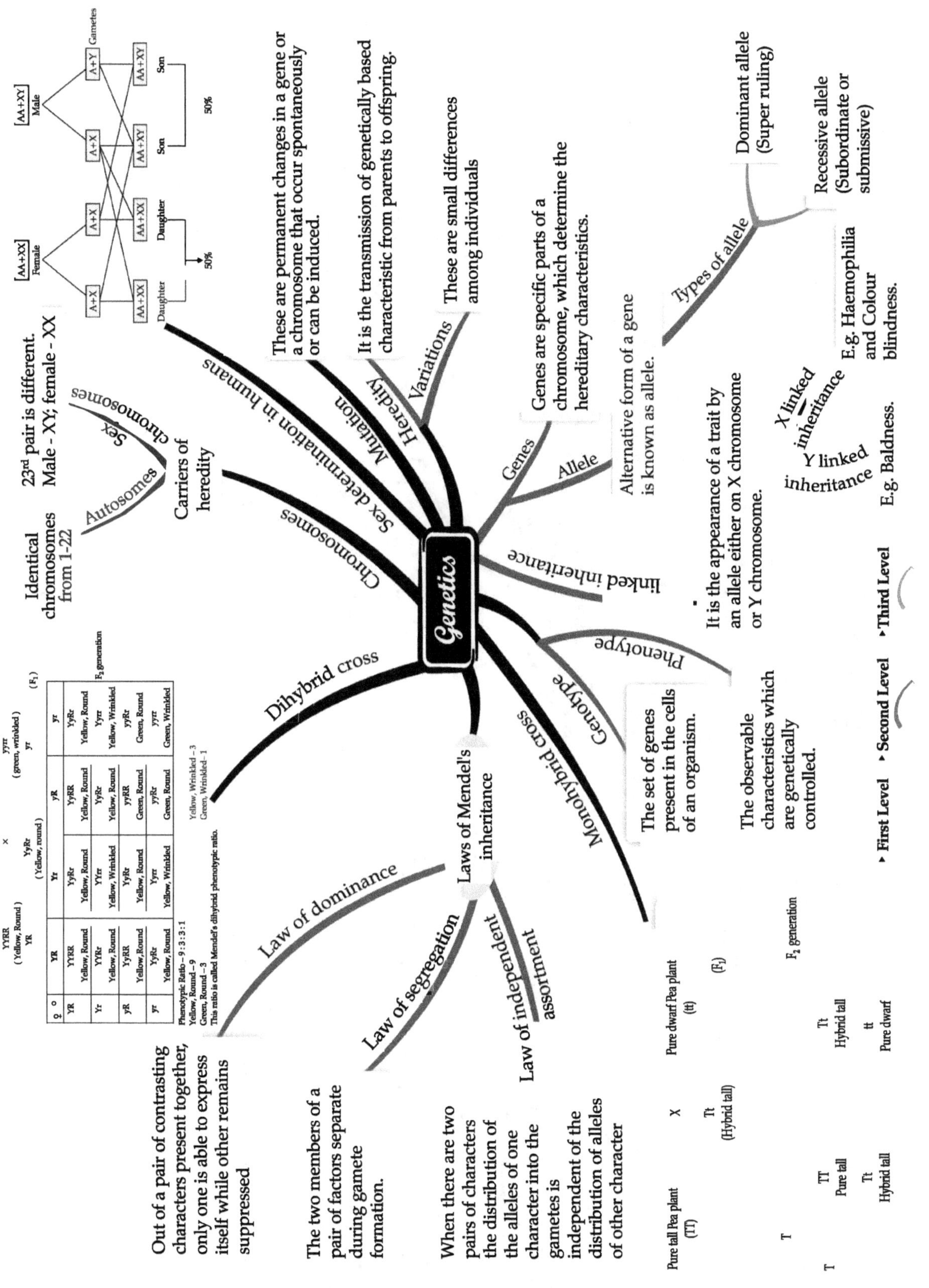

Genetics

Chromosomes
- Carriers of heredity
- Autosomes: Identical chromosomes from 1-22
- Sex chromosomes: 23rd pair is different. Male - XY; female - XX

Sex determination in humans

[AA+XX] Female × [AA+XY] Male

Gametes: A+X, A+X, A+X, A+Y

AA+XX Daughter, AA+XX Daughter, AA+XY Son, AA+XY Son

50% 50%

Mutation
- These are permanent changes in a gene or a chromosome that occur spontaneously or can be induced.

Heredity
- It is the transmission of genetically based characteristic from parents to offspring.

Variations
- These are small differences among individuals

Genes
- Genes are specific parts of a chromosome, which determine the hereditary characteristics.

Allele
- Alternative form of a gene is known as allele.
- Types of allele
  - Dominant allele (Super ruling)
  - Recessive allele (Subordinate or submissive)

linked inheritance
- It is the appearance of a trait by an allele either on X chromosome or Y chromosome.
- X linked inheritance: E.g. Haemophilia and Colour blindness.
- Y linked inheritance: E.g. Baldness.

Phenotype
- The observable characteristics which are genetically controlled.

Genotype
- The set of genes present in the cells of an organism.

Monohybrid cross

Pure tall Pea plant (TT) X Pure dwarf Pea plant (tt)

Tt (Hybrid tall) (F1)

T T

F2 generation

TT Pure tall, Tt Hybrid tall, Tt Hybrid tall, tt Pure dwarf

Laws of Mendel's inheritance
- Law of dominance: Out of a pair of contrasting characters present together, only one is able to express itself while other remains suppressed
- Law of segregation: The two members of a pair of factors separate during gamete formation.
- Law of independent assortment: When there are two pairs of characters the distribution of the alleles of one character into the gametes is independent of the distribution of alleles of other character

Dihybrid cross

YYRR (Yellow, Round) YR × yyrr (green, wrinkled) yr

YyRr (Yellow, round) (F1)

♀ ♂	YR	Yr	yR	yr
YR	YYRR Yellow, Round	YyRr Yellow, Round	YyRR Yellow, Round	YyRr Yellow, Round
Yr	YYRr Yellow, Round	YYrr Yellow, Wrinkled	YyRr Yellow, Round	Yyrr Yellow, Wrinkled
yR	YyRR Yellow,Round	YyRr Yellow, Round	yyRR Green, Round	yyRr Green, Round
yr	YyRr Yellow, Round	Yyrr Yellow, Wrinkled	yyRr Green, Round	yyrr Green, Wrinkled

F_2 generation

Phenotypic Ratio – 9 : 3 : 3 : 1
Yellow, Round – 9
Green, Round – 3
Yellow, Wrinkled – 3
Green, Wrinkled – 1
This ratio is called Mendel's dihybrid phenotypic ratio.

▸ First Level ▸ Second Level ▸ Third Level

Mind Map :Absorption by roots

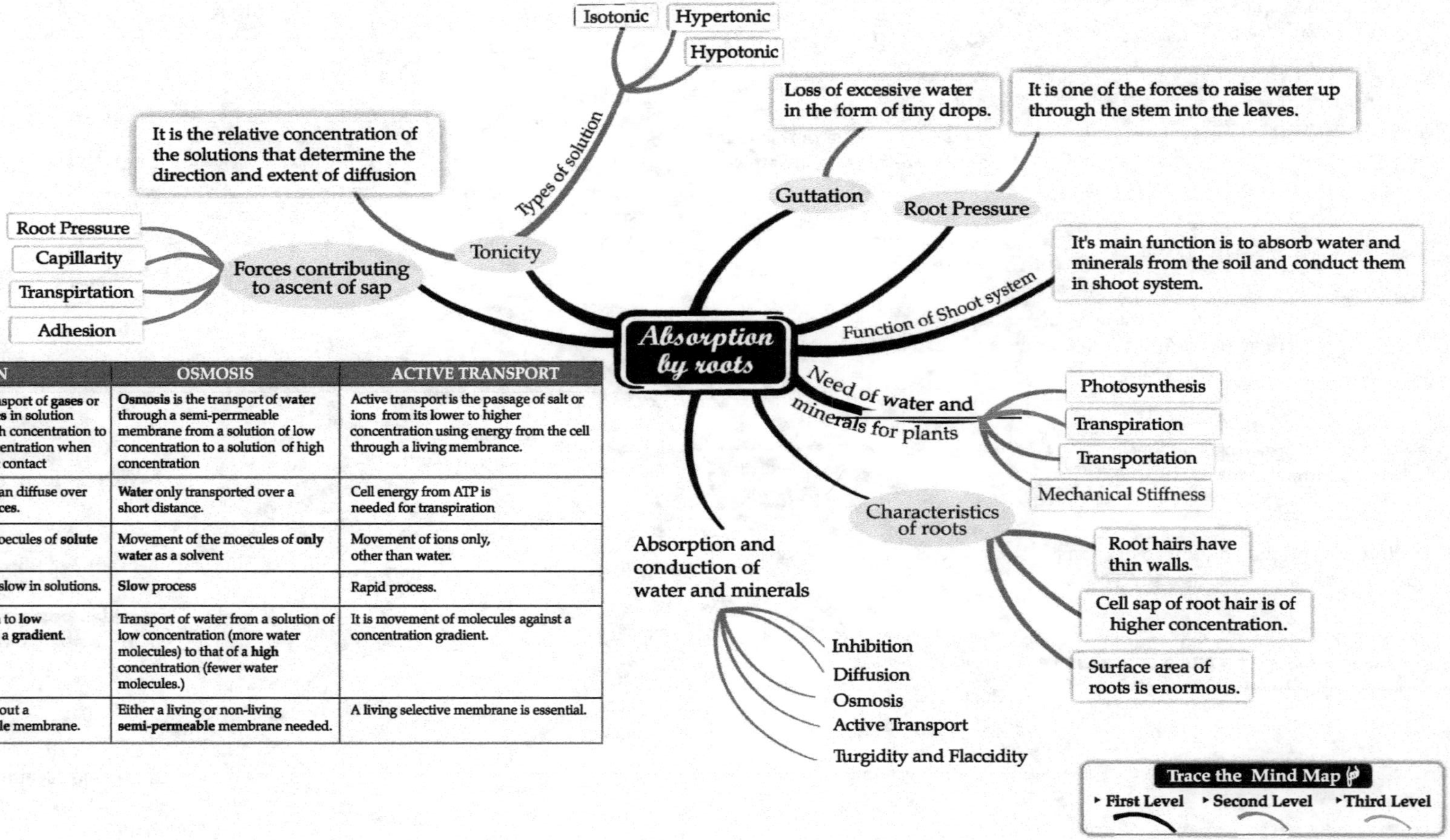

Absorption by roots

- **Forces contributing to ascent of sap**
  - Root Pressure
  - Capillarity
  - Transpirtation
  - Adhesion
- **Tonicity**
  - It is the relative concentration of the solutions that determine the direction and extent of diffusion
  - Types of solution
    - Isotonic
    - Hypertonic
    - Hypotonic
- **Guttation**
  - Loss of excessive water in the form of tiny drops.
- **Root Pressure**
  - It is one of the forces to raise water up through the stem into the leaves.
- **Function of Shoot system**
  - It's main function is to absorb water and minerals from the soil and conduct them in shoot system.
- **Need of water and minerals for plants**
  - Photosynthesis
  - Transpiration
  - Transportation
  - Mechanical Stiffness
- **Characteristics of roots**
  - Root hairs have thin walls.
  - Cell sap of root hair is of higher concentration.
  - Surface area of roots is enormous.
- **Absorption and conduction of water and minerals**
  - Inhibition
  - Diffusion
  - Osmosis
  - Active Transport
  - Turgidity and Flaccidity

DIFFUSION	OSMOSIS	ACTIVE TRANSPORT
1. **Diffusion** is the transport of **gases** or **dissolved substances** in solution from a region of high concentration to a region of low concentration when the two are in direct contact	**Osmosis** is the transport of **water** through a semi-perrmeable membrane from a solution of low concentration to a solution of high concentration	Active transport is the passage of salt or ions from its lower to higher concentration using energy from the cell through a living membrance.
2. **Liquids** and **gases** can diffuse over **considerable distances.**	**Water** only transported over a short distance.	Cell energy from ATP is needed for transpiration
3. Movement of the moecules of **solute** or **solvent.**	Movement of the moecules of **only water** as a solvent	Movement of ions only, other than water.
4. **Rapid in gases,** but slow in solutions.	**Slow** process	Rapid process.
5. Transport from **high** to **low** concentration along a **gradient.**	Transport of water from a solution of low concentration (more water molecules) to that of a **high** concentration (fewer water molecules.)	It is movement of molecules against a concentration gradient.
6. Occurs with or without a non-living **permeable** membrane.	Either a living or non-living **semi-permeable** membrane needed.	A living selective membrane is essential.

Trace the Mind Map
- First Level
- Second Level
- Third Level

Mind Map : Photosynthesis

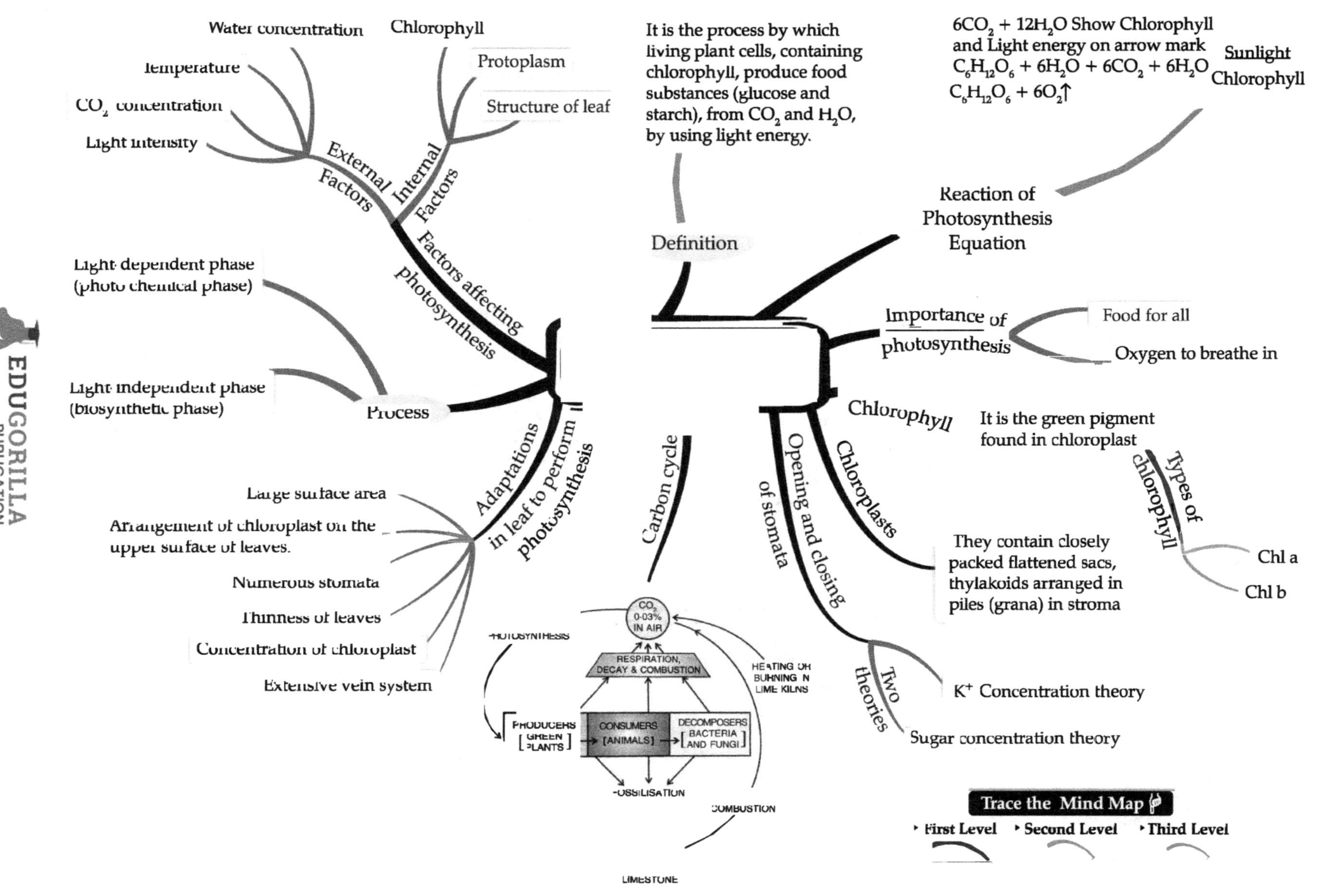

Mind Map : Chemical coordination in Plants

Phytohormone (Plant hormones)

Plants respond to stimuli by producing chemicals known as plant hormones.

Types
- Auxins
- Gibberellins
- Cytokinins
- Ethylene
- Abscisic acid

Stimuli and response

Internal environment of an organism are called stimuli and the resulting actions or the movements caused by the stimuli are called responses.

Tropism

Definition: Plant movements in response to stimuli from some direction like light, gravity, chemicals and water are called tropism.

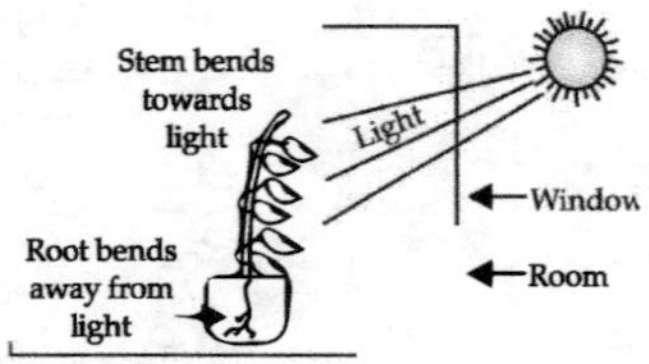

Types
- Thigmotropism — Movement in response to touch or stimulus
- Chemotropism — Movement in response to chemicals
- Hydrotropism — Movement in response to water
- Geotropism — Growth towards earth's gravity
- Phototropism — Movement towards light

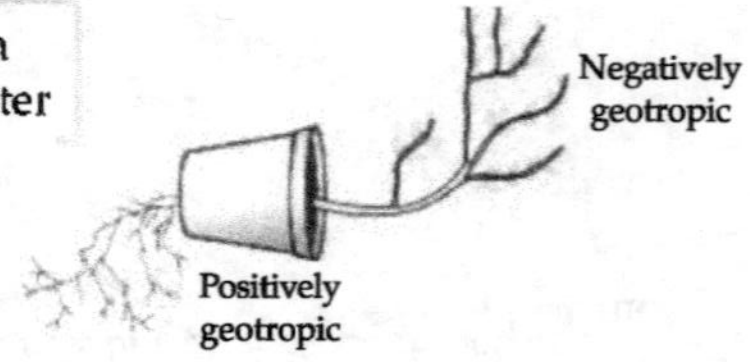

Stem bends towards light
Light
Window
Room
Root bends away from light

Negatively geotropic
Positively geotropic

Plant hormone	Site of synthesis	Functions
1. **Auxins**	• Synthesized primarily in shoot apical meristems and young leaves.	• Promote cell elongation. • Suppress the growth of lateral buds. • Delay fall of leaves • Induce formation of parthenocarpic fruits.
2. **Gibberellins**	• Synthesized primarily in the meristems of apical buds and roots.	• Help in stem-elongation. • Break dormancy of seeds and buds. • Delay senescence. • Induce parthenocarpy.
3. **Cytokinins**	• Synthesized primarily in roots and transported to other organs.	• Stimulate cell-division and cell enlargement • Prevent ageing of plant parts. • Inhibit apical dominance
4. **Ethylene**	• Synthesized in senescent leaves and flowers, germinating seeds and ripening fruits.	• Induces fruit ripening. • Promotes sencscene
5. **Abscisic acid**	• Synthesized in green fruits and seeds at the begining of the winter period.	• Induces dormancy of buds and seeds. • Inhibits seed-germination and development. • Stimulates closing of stomata.

▸ **First Level** ▸ **Second Level** ▸ **Third Level**

Mind Map : Circulatory system

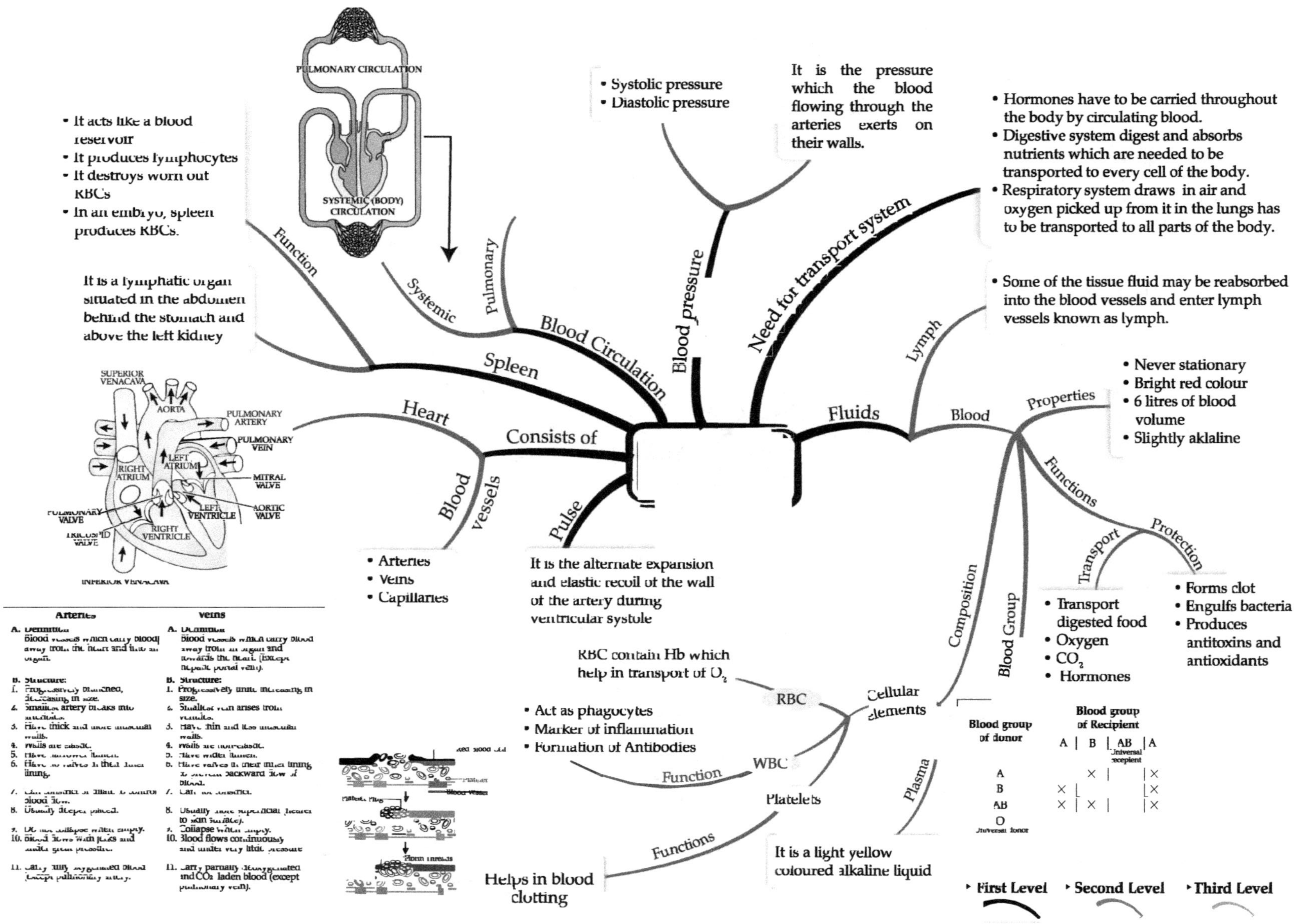

Need for transport system
- Hormones have to be carried throughout the body by circulating blood.
- Digestive system digest and absorbs nutrients which are needed to be transported to every cell of the body.
- Respiratory system draws in air and oxygen picked up from it in the lungs has to be transported to all parts of the body.

Blood pressure
It is the pressure which the blood flowing through the arteries exerts on their walls.

- Systolic pressure
- Diastolic pressure

Blood Circulation
- Pulmonary
- Systemic

PULMONARY CIRCULATION

SYSTEMIC (BODY) CIRCULATION

Fluids
Lymph
- Some of the tissue fluid may be reabsorbed into the blood vessels and enter lymph vessels known as lymph.

Blood
Properties
- Never stationary
- Bright red colour
- 6 litres of blood volume
- Slightly aklaline

Functions

Transport
- Transport digested food
- Oxygen
- CO_2
- Hormones

Protection
- Forms clot
- Engulfs bacteria
- Produces antitoxins and antioxidants

Blood Group

Blood group of donor	Blood group of Recipient: A	B	AB (Universal recepient)	A
A		×		×
B	×			×
AB	×	×		×
O (Universal donor)				

Composition

Plasma
- It is a light yellow coloured alkaline liquid

Cellular elements
- RBC: RBC contain Hb which help in transport of O_2
- WBC — Function:
  - Act as phagocytes
  - Marker of inflammation
  - Formation of Antibodies
- Platelets — Functions: Helps in blood clotting

Platelet Plug

Fibrin threads

Pulse
It is the alternate expansion and elastic recoil of the wall of the artery during ventricular systole

Consists of
Heart
SUPERIOR VENACAVA

AORTA

PULMONARY ARTERY

PULMONARY VEIN

LEFT ATRIUM

RIGHT ATRIUM

MITRAL VALVE

AORTIC VALVE

LEFT VENTRICLE

RIGHT VENTRICLE

PULMONARY VALVE

TRICUSPID VALVE

INFERIOR VENACAVA

Blood vessels
- Arteries
- Veins
- Capillaries

Arteries	Veins
A. Definition: Blood vessels which carry blood away from the heart and into an organ.	A. Definition: Blood vessels which carry blood away from an organ and towards the heart. (Except hepatic portal vein).
B. Structure:	B. Structure:
1. Progressively branched, decreasing in size.	1. Progressively unite increasing in size.
2. Smallest artery breaks into arterioles.	2. Smallest vein arises from venules.
3. Have thick and more muscular walls.	3. Have thin and less muscular walls.
4. Walls are elastic.	4. Walls are non-elastic.
5. Have narrower lumen.	5. Have wider lumen.
6. Have no valves in their inner lining.	6. Have valves in their inner lining to prevent backward flow of blood.
7. Can constrict or dilate to control blood flow.	7. Can not constrict.
8. Usually deeper placed.	8. Usually more superficial (nearer to skin surface).
9. Do not collapse when empty.	9. Collapse when empty.
10. Blood flows with jerks and under great pressure.	10. Blood flows continuously and under very little pressure
11. Carry fully oxygenated blood (except pulmonary artery).	11. Carry partially deoxygenated and CO_2 laden blood (except pulmonary vein).

Spleen
It is a lymphatic organ situated in the abdomen behind the stomach and above the left kidney

Function
- It acts like a blood reservoir
- It produces lymphocytes
- It destroys worn out RBCs
- In an embryo, spleen produces RBCs.

First Level | Second Level | Third Level

Mind Map : Excretory system

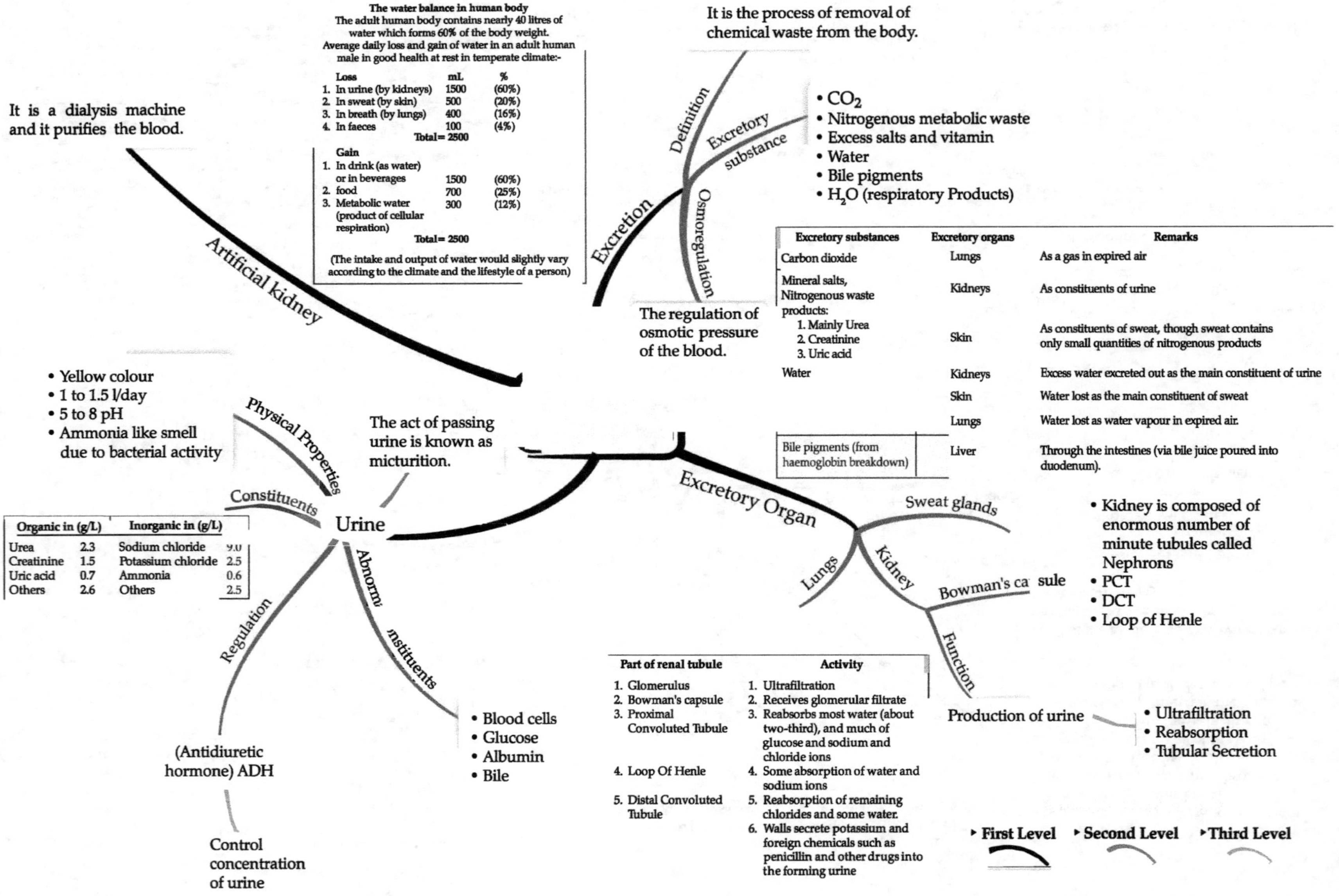

Excretion

Definition: It is the process of removal of chemical waste from the body.

Excretory substance:

- CO_2
- Nitrogenous metabolic waste
- Excess salts and vitamin
- Water
- Bile pigments
- H_2O (respiratory Products)

Osmoregulation: The regulation of osmotic pressure of the blood.

Excretory substances	Excretory organs	Remarks
Carbon dioxide	Lungs	As a gas in expired air
Mineral salts, Nitrogenous waste products: 1. Mainly Urea 2. Creatinine 3. Uric acid	Kidneys	As constituents of urine
	Skin	As constituents of sweat, though sweat contains only small quantities of nitrogenous products
Water	Kidneys	Excess water excreted out as the main constituent of urine
	Skin	Water lost as the main constituent of sweat
	Lungs	Water lost as water vapour in expired air.
Bile pigments (from haemoglobin breakdown)	Liver	Through the intestines (via bile juice poured into duodenum).

Artificial kidney

It is a dialysis machine and it purifies the blood.

The water balance in human body

The adult human body contains nearly 40 litres of water which forms 60% of the body weight.

Average daily loss and gain of water in an adult human male in good health at rest in temperate climate:-

Loss	mL	%
1. In urine (by kidneys)	1500	(60%)
2. In sweat (by skin)	500	(20%)
3. In breath (by lungs)	400	(16%)
4. In faeces	100	(4%)
Total= 2500		

Gain		
1. In drink (as water) or in beverages	1500	(60%)
2. food	700	(25%)
3. Metabolic water (product of cellular respiration)	300	(12%)
Total= 2500		

(The intake and output of water would slightly vary according to the climate and the lifestyle of a person)

Excretory Organ

- Lungs
- Sweat glands
- Kidney
  - Kidney is composed of enormous number of minute tubules called Nephrons
    - Bowman's capsule
    - PCT
    - DCT
    - Loop of Henle
  - Function: Production of urine
    - Ultrafiltration
    - Reabsorption
    - Tubular Secretion

Part of renal tubule	Activity
1. Glomerulus	1. Ultrafiltration
2. Bowman's capsule	2. Receives glomerular filtrate
3. Proximal Convoluted Tubule	3. Reabsorbs most water (about two-third), and much of glucose and sodium and chloride ions
4. Loop Of Henle	4. Some absorption of water and sodium ions
5. Distal Convoluted Tubule	5. Reabsorption of remaining chlorides and some water. 6. Walls secrete potassium and foreign chemicals such as penicillin and other drugs into the forming urine

Urine

The act of passing urine is known as micturition.

Physical Properties:

- Yellow colour
- 1 to 1.5 l/day
- 5 to 8 pH
- Ammonia like smell due to bacterial activity

Constituents:

Organic in (g/L)		Inorganic in (g/L)	
Urea	2.3	Sodium chloride	9.0
Creatinine	1.5	Potassium chloride	2.5
Uric acid	0.7	Ammonia	0.6
Others	2.6	Others	2.5

Abnormal constituents:

- Blood cells
- Glucose
- Albumin
- Bile

Regulation: (Antidiuretic hormone) ADH — Control concentration of urine

▸ First Level ▸ Second Level ▸ Third Level

Mind Map : Nervous System

Reflex action

Definition: It is automatic involuntary action of our body brought about by stimulus

Reflexes (Involuntary actions)	Voluntary actions
1. Initiated by some stimulus (touch, pain, pressure, heat, light, etc.)	1. Initiated by a willing thought.
2. Mainly self protective dueto environment.	2. Fulfilment of a desired goal.
3. Commands originate mostly in the spinal cord and autonomic nervous system and a few in the brain as well.	3. Commands originate in brain.
4. Involve muscles and glands.	4. Involveonly muscles.

Type:
- Natural
- Conditioned

Natural (Simple) Reflex	Conditioned (Acquired) Reflex
1. Inborn (inherited) requiring no previous experience.	1. Developed by experience or learning.
2. Directly related to the stimulus	2. Brought about by a condition totally different from the direct initial stimulus.
3. Similar in all humans (or similar among all individuals of any one species)	3. Differs in different individuals, subject to learning and experience

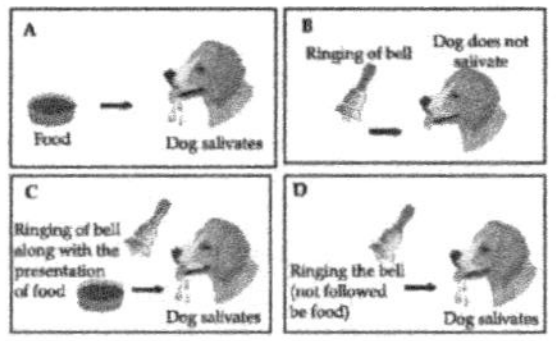

A: Food → Dog salivates
B: Ringing of bell → Dog does not salivate
C: Ringing of bell along with the presentation of food → Dog salivates
D: Ringing the bell (not followed be food) → Dog salivates

Reflex arc

It is the shortest route that can be taken by an reception to an effector.

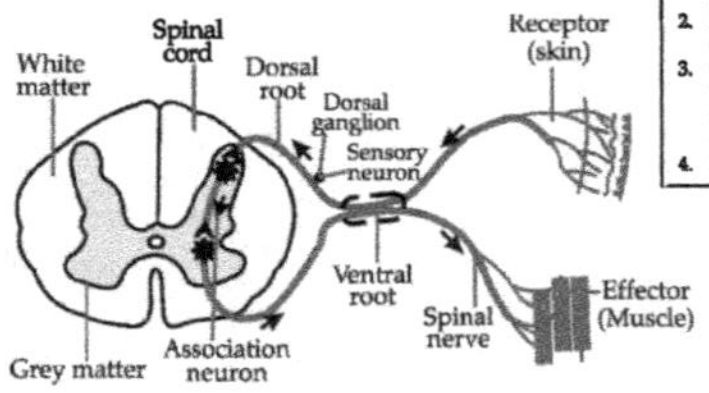

Need of nervous system

- Keep us informed about the outside world
- Enable us to remember, to think and to reason out
- Controls all voluntary muscular activities.
- Regulates involuntary activities.

Neuron

Definition: It is the structural and functional unit of nervous system

Part:
- Cell body
- Dendrite
- Axon

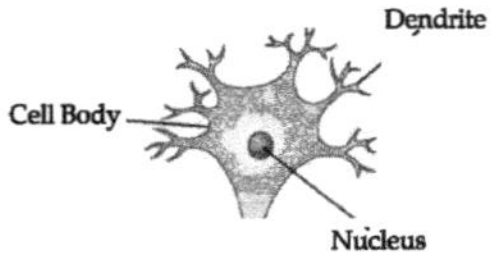

Dendrite, Cell Body, Nucleus, Axon

Types:
- Sensory
- Motor
- Association

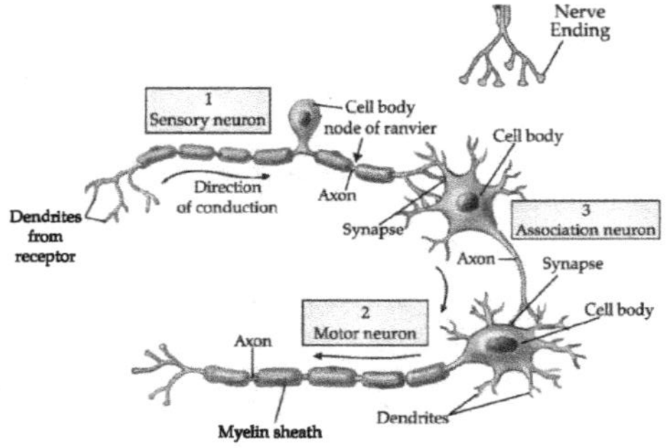

Nerve Ending; 1 Sensory neuron; Cell body; node of ranvier; Direction of conduction; Dendrites from receptor; Axon; Synapse; Cell body; 3 Association neuron; Axon; Synapse; Cell body; 2 Motor neuron; Axon; Myelin sheath; Dendrites

Transmission of Nerve Impulse

A: Resting region (Polarised)

B: Excited region (Depolarisation); Resting region

C: Recovery region (Repolarisation); Excited region; Resting region

Synapse

It is the point of contact between the terminal branches of the axon of a neuron with the dendrites of other neuron separated by a fine gap.

Nerves

Nerve is a bundle of fibers in the body.

Type:
- Sensory: Bring impulses from the receptors to the brain or spinal cord.
- Motor: Carry impulse from the brain or spinal cord to effector organs.
- Mixed: They contain both sensory and motor fibres.

Actions

- Voluntary: Performed consciously
- Involuntary: Performed inconsciously

Component

Nervous System

- Central Nervous System (CNS)
  - Brain
    - Cerebrum: Controls conscious and unconscious mind, intelligence, memory, reason, etc.
    - Cerebellum: Maintains balance of body.
    - Medulla oblongata: Controls involuntary actions - heartbeat breathing, peristalsis
  - Spinal Cord: Controls reflex actions, conveys impulses
- Peripheral Nervous System (PNS)
  - Somatic Nervous System
    - Cranialnerves (12 pairs)
    - Spinalnerve (31 pairs)
  - Autonomic Nervous System (ANS) (Pair of chains of ganglia, close to or embedded in the organs.)
    - Sympathetic (nerves between neck and waist) (Stimulatory) Acceleratesheart beat, dilates pupil, constricts blood vessels, releasessugar fromliver.
    - Parasympathetic (Nerves above neck and below sacrum) (Calming) Restores normal body condition

White matter, Spinal cord, Dorsal root, Dorsal ganglion, Sensory neuron, Receptor (skin), Ventral root, Spinal nerve, Effector (Muscle), Grey matter, Association neuron

First Level · Second Level · Third Level

Mind Map : Endocrine System

The regulation of the quantity of the hormones and the timing of its release is controlled by feedback mechanism.

Source		Hormones and their action
Anterior pituitary	GROWTH HORMONE (GH)	*Promotes growth of whole body, particularly of the skeleton* *Deficiency (-) in childhood = Dwarfism* *Excess: (+) In childhood = Gigantism* *In adult = Acromegaly*
	TROPIC HORMONES (Stimulate certain other endocrine glands)	*THYROID STIMULATING HORMONE (TSH) (Stimulates thyroid to secrete thyroxine)* *ADRENOCORTICOTROPIC HORMONE (ACTH) (Stimulates adrenal cortex)* *GONADOTROPIC HORMONES (Regulate the activities of Gonads-testes and ovaries) These are mainly of three types:* *(i) Follicle-Stimulating hormone (FSH). Stimulates egg formation in females and sperm formation in males* *(ii) Luteinizing hormone (LH). Stimulates the formation of corpus luteum to produce the female hormone progesterone, and the testes to produce the male hormone testosterone* *(iii) Prolactin - Milk secretion*
Posterior pituitary	ANTIDIURETIC HORMONE (ADH) or vasopressin	*Increases reabsorption of water from kidney tubules* *Deficiency : Diabetes insipidus (water diabetes)*
	OXYTOCIN	*Uterine contraction during child birth, stimulates milk ejection*

Feedback Mechanism

- Positive feedback — Ex- Uterine contractions during childbirth
- Negative feedback — Ex- TSH level

Endocrine system secrete hormones. These are extremely important secretion for the regulation of body activity.

Hormones

Hormonal control	Nervous control
• Usually **slow**. • Transmitted **chemically** through blood. • Affect **different organs (widespread** in body) • Effect is **short term of long-lasting.** • **Can affect growth.** • Can bring about specific chemical changes and **regulates metabolism.** • **Cannot be modified** by learning from previous experience.	• Immediate/**Rapid.** • Transmitted **electro chemically** through the nerve fiber and chemically across synapses. • Affect only the particular muscles or the glands **(local)** • Effect is **only short-lived.** • **Cannot affect growth.** • Does not influence chemical changes and **cannot regulate metabolism.** • **Can be modified** to some extent by learning from previous experience.

- Secreted directly into the blood
- Regulated by chemical means
- Act on target organs
- Biologically very active

	Body part	Effects of adrenaline	Biological advantage	Effect of sensation
1	Heart	Beats faster Blood pressure increases	Sends more glucose and oxygen to the muscles	Thumping heart
2	Breathing centre of the brain	Faster and deeper breathing	Increased oxygenation of the blood; rapid removal of carbon dioxide	Panting
3	Arterioles of the skin	Constricts them	Less blood going to the skin means more is available to the muscles	Person turns pale
4	Arterioles of the digestive system	Constricts them	Less blood to the digestive system, allows more blood to reach the muscles	Dry mouth
5	Muscles of body	Tenses them	Ready for immediate action	Tense feeling, shivering
6	Liver	Conversion of glycogen to glucose	Glucose available in blood for energy production	No sensation
7	Fat deposit	Conversion of fats into fatty acids	Fatty acids available in blood, for muscles contraction	No sensation

Endocrine glands

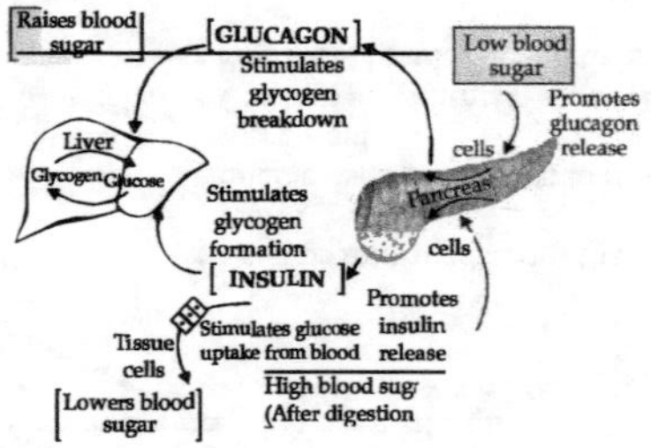

- **Pituitary (Master gland)**
  - Anterior Pituitary
  - Posterior Pituitary
  - It is a small projection which hangs from the base of the mid-brain below hypothalamus
- **Adrenal**
  - Adrenal medulla — Secretes adrenaline
  - Adrenal cortex — Secretes cortisone
- **Pancreas**
  - Insulin
  - Glucagon

- **Thyroid**
  - Calcitonin
  - Thyroxine
    - Regulates
      - Basal metabolism
      - Body temperature
      - Growth
    - Under Secretion
      - Myxedema — In adults if thyroid doesn't function properly, person becomes sluggish
      - Cretinism — In children causes Dwarfism and mental retardation
      - Simple Goitre — Enlargement of thyroid
    - Oversecretion
      - Shortness of breath
      - Eyes are protruded
      - Exophthalmic Goitre (exo : outward, ophthalmos : eye)
      - Rapid heart beat

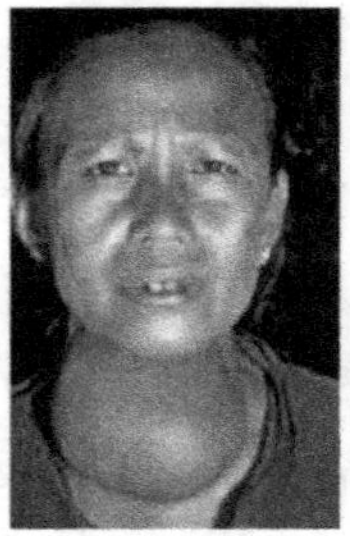

▸ First Level ▸ Second Level ▸ Third Level

Mind Map : Reproductive system

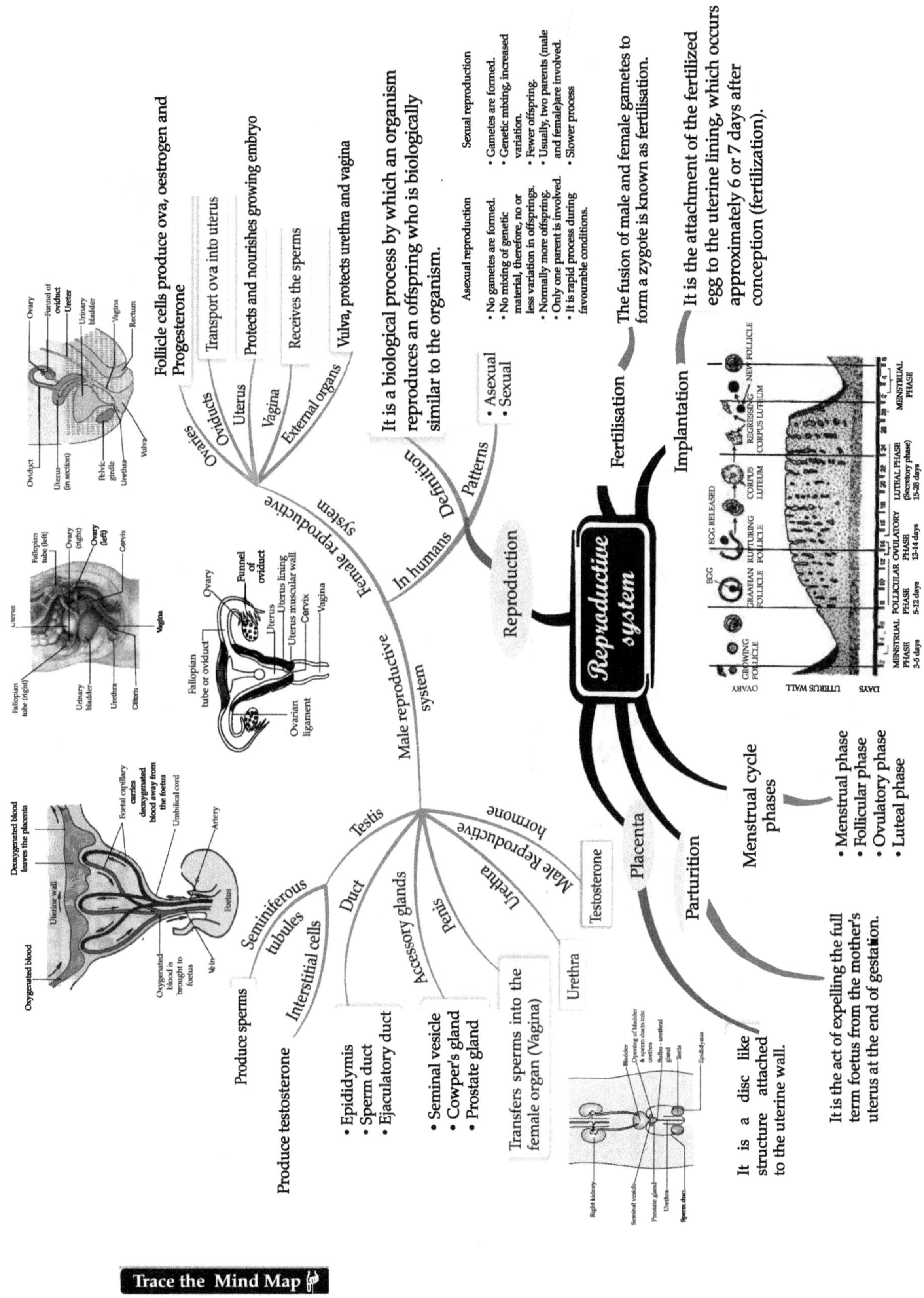

Reproductive system

Reproduction

- **In humans**
  - **Female reproductive system**
    - Ovaries — Follicle cells produce ova, oestrogen and Progesterone
    - Oviducts — Transport ova into uterus
    - Uterus — Protects and nourishes growing embryo
    - Vagina — Receives the sperms
    - External organs — Vulva, protects urethra and vagina
  - **Male reproductive system**
    - Testis
      - Seminiferous tubules — Produce sperms
      - Interstitial cells — Produce testosterone
    - Duct
      - Epididymis
      - Sperm duct
      - Ejaculatory duct
    - Accessory glands
      - Seminal vesicle
      - Cowper's gland
      - Prostate gland
    - Penis — Transfers sperms into the female organ (Vagina)
    - Urethra — Urethra
    - Male Reproductive hormone — Testosterone
- **Definition** — It is a biological process by which an organism reproduces an offspring who is biologically similar to the organism.
- **Patterns**
  - Asexual
  - Sexual

Asexual reproduction	Sexual reproduction
• No gametes are formed. • No mixing of genetic material, therefore, no or less variation in offsprings. • Normally more offspring. • Only one parent is involved. • It is rapid process during favourable conditions.	• Gametes are formed. • Genetic mixing, increased variation. • Fewer offspring. • Usually, two parents (male and female)are involved. • Slower process

Fertilisation

The fusion of male and female gametes to form a zygote is known as fertilisation.

Implantation

It is the attachment of the fertilized egg to the uterine lining, which occurs approximately 6 or 7 days after conception (fertilization).

Menstrual cycle phases

- Menstrual phase
- Follicular phase
- Ovulatory phase
- Luteal phase

Parturition

It is the act of expelling the full term foetus from the mother's uterus at the end of gestation.

Placenta

It is a disc like structure attached to the uterine wall.

Trace the Mind Map

- First Level
- Second Le
- Third Level

Mind Map : Population

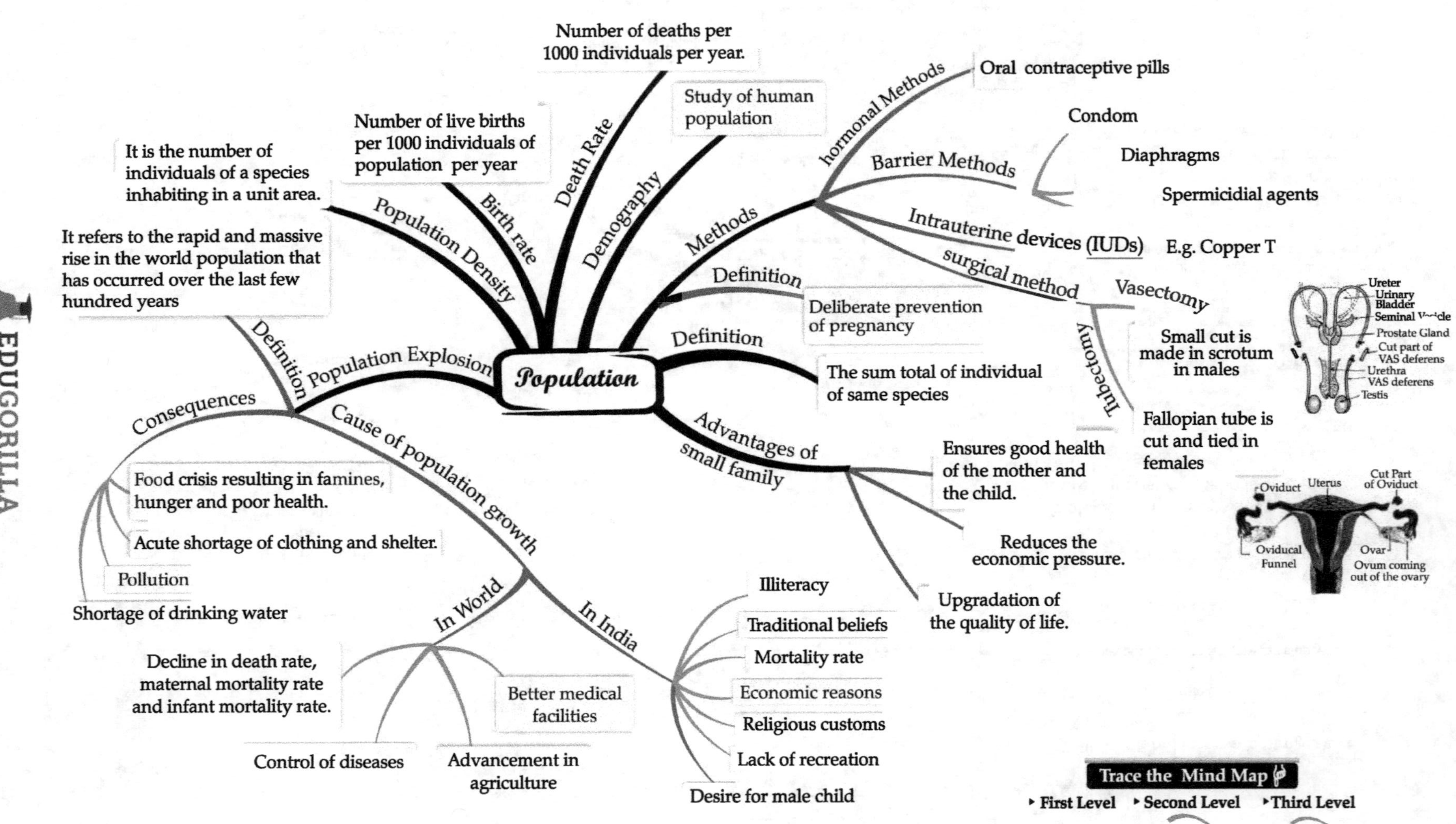

Mind Map : Human Evolution

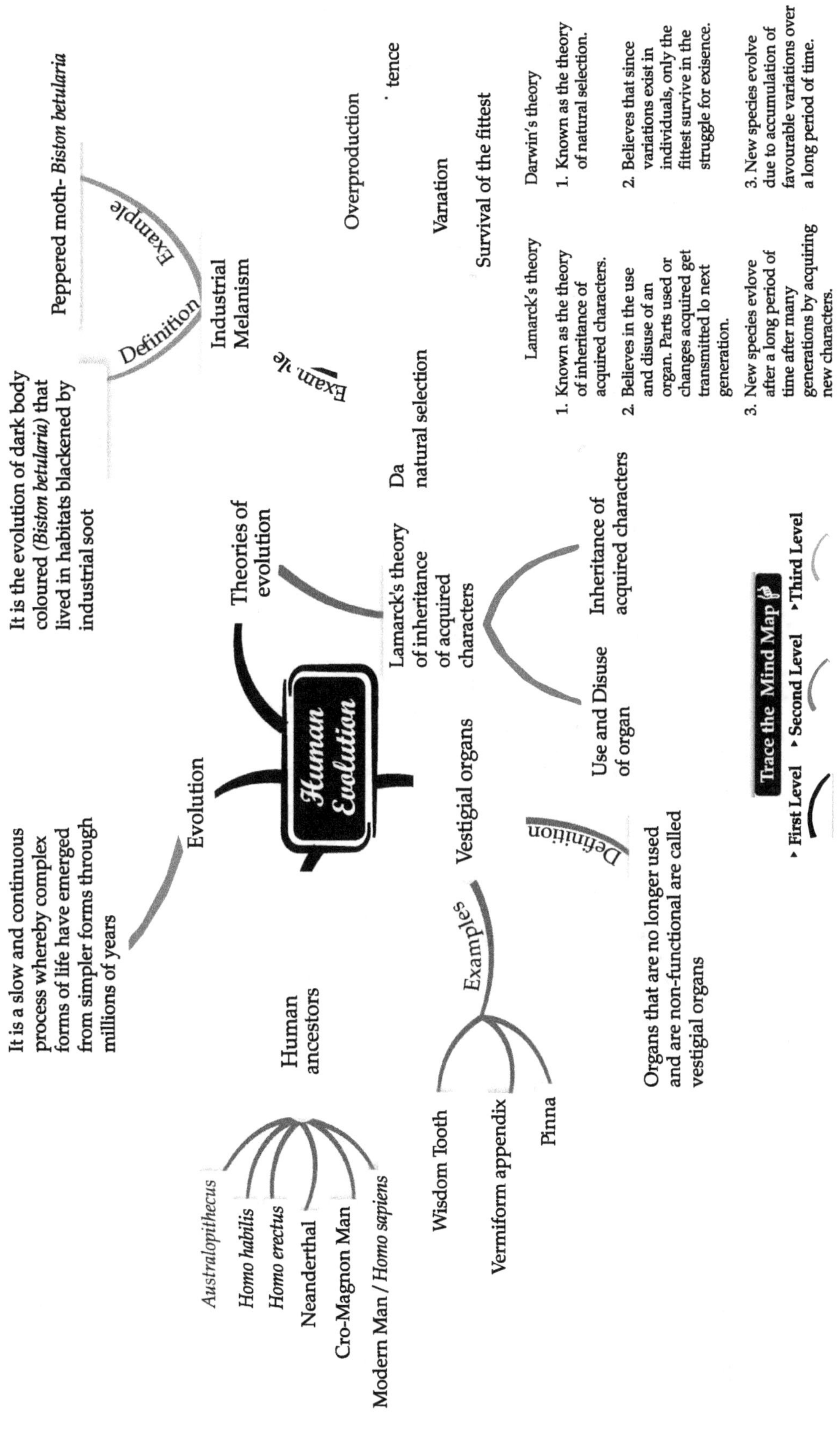

Human Evolution

Evolution

It is a slow and continuous process whereby complex forms of life have emerged from simpler forms through millions of years

Theories of evolution

Industrial Melanism

Definition: It is the evolution of dark body coloured *(Biston betularia)* that lived in habitats blackened by industrial soot

Example: Peppered moth- *Biston betularia*

Exam. le

Da
natural selection

Overproduction

· tence

Variation

Survival of the fittest

Lamarck's theory of inheritance of acquired characters

- Use and Disuse of organ
- Inheritance of acquired characters

Lamarck's theory	Darwin's theory
1. Known as the theory of inheritance of acquired characters.	1. Known as the theory of natural selection.
2. Believes in the use and disuse of an organ. Parts used or changes acquired get transmitted lo next generation.	2. Believes that since variations exist in individuals, only the fittest survive in the struggle for exisence.
3. New species evlove after a long period of time after many generations by acquiring new characters.	3. New species evolve due to accumulation of favourable variations over a long period of time.

Human ancestors

- *Australopithecus*
- *Homo habilis*
- *Homo erectus*
- Neanderthal
- Cro-Magnon Man
- Modern Man / *Homo sapiens*

Vestigial organs

Definition: Organs that are no longer used and are non-functional are called vestigial organs

Examples:

- Wisdom Tooth
- Vermiform appendix
- Pinna

Trace the Mind Map

‣ First Level ‣ Second Level ‣ Third Level

Mind Map : Pollution

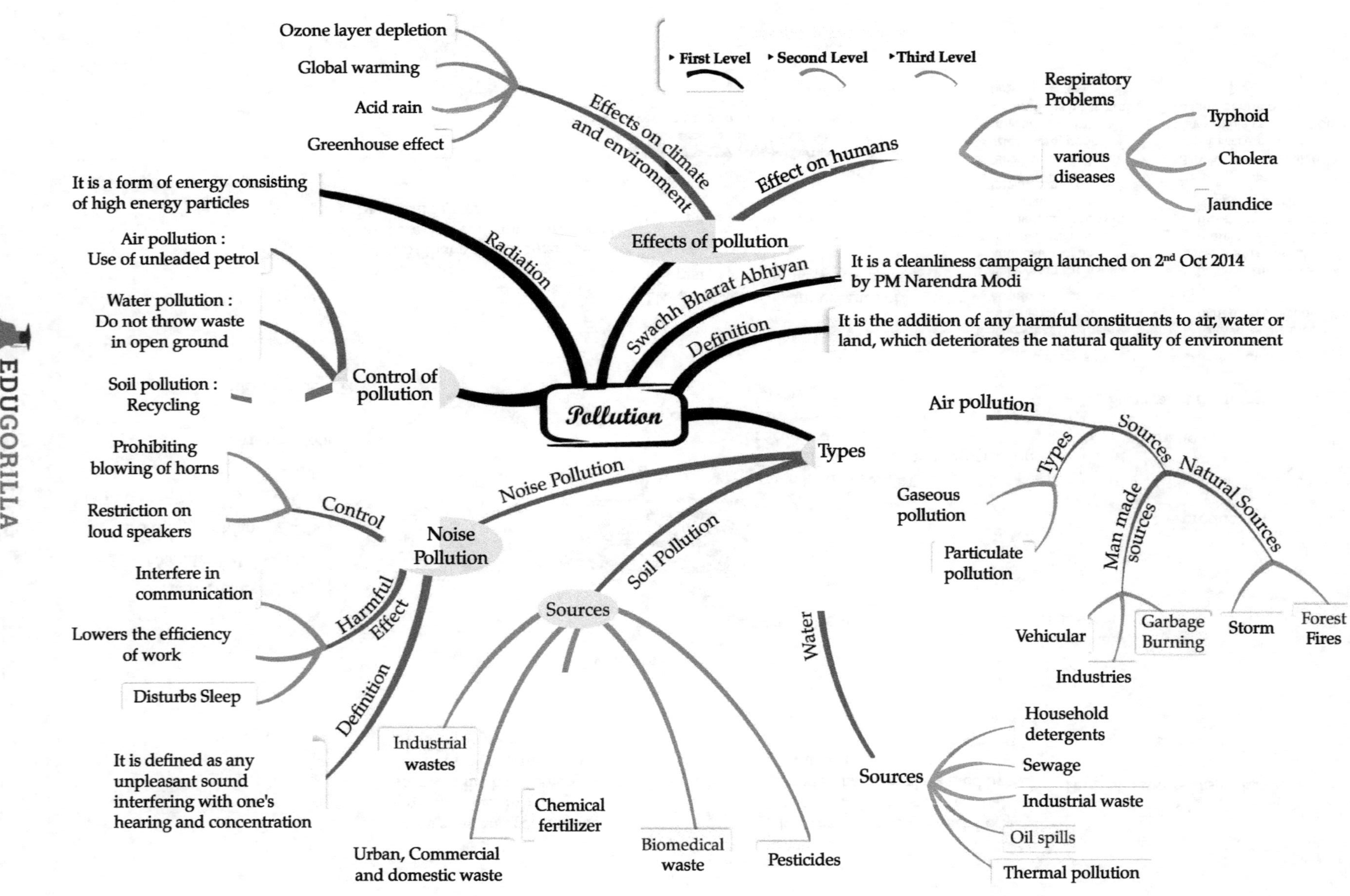

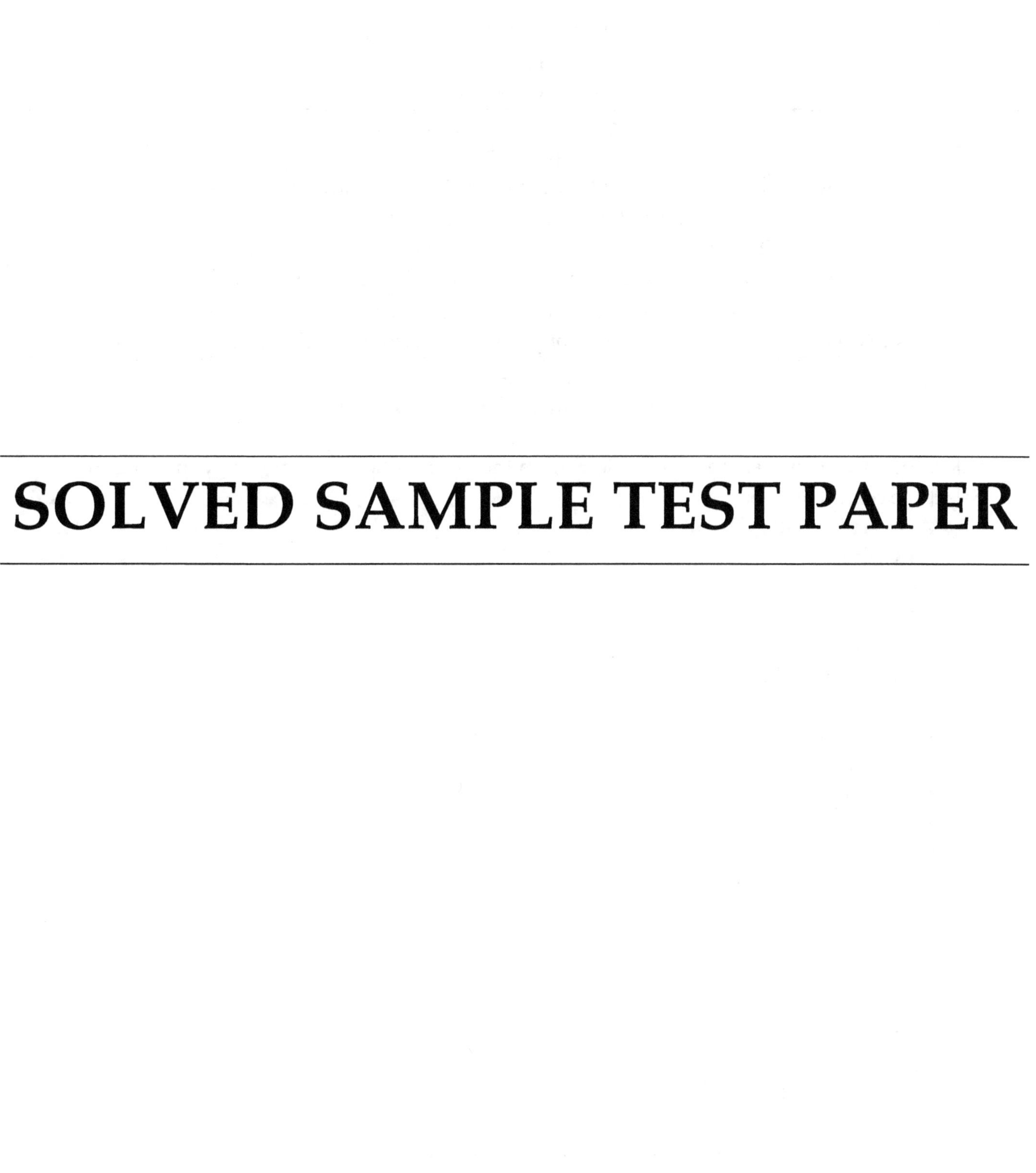

SOLVED SAMPLE TEST PAPER

ICSE 2023 EXAMINATION

SPECIMEN QUESTION PAPER

BIOLOGY

(SCIENCE PAPER-2)

Maximum Marks: 80

Time allowed: Two hours

Answers to this Paper must be written on the paper provided separately.

You will not be allowed to write during first 15 minutes.

This time is to be spent in reading the question paper.

The time given at the head of this Paper is the time allowed for writing the answers.

(Section A is compulsory. Attempt any four questions from Section B.

The intended marks for questions or parts of questions are given in brackets [ ].

Section A

Answer all the questions from this section

Question 1.

Select the correct answers to the questions from the given options. (Do not copy the question. Select the correct answer only **[15]**

(i) A muscular wall is absent in:

(a) Capillary

(b) Arteriole

(c) Venule

(d) Vein

Answer: (a) Capillary

(ii) On which day of the menstrual cycle does ovulation take place?

(a) 1 st day

(b) 5th day

(c) 14th day

(d) 28th day

Answer: (c) 14th day

(iii) Ganong's Photometer is used to study:

(a) Photosynthesis

(b) Rate of uptake of water

(c) Exosmosis

(d) Guttation

Answer: (b) Rate of uptake of water

(iv) The number of chromosomes in a human skin cell are:

(a) 22

(b) 23

(c) 44

(d) 46
Answer: (d) 46

(v) Cretinism and Myxedema are due to:
(a) Hypersecretion of thyroxine
(b) Hypersecretion of growth hormone
(c) Hyposecretion of thyroxine
(d) Hypersecretion of growth hormone
Answer: (c) Hyposecretion of thyroxine

(vi) A light-dependent phase of photosynthesis in green leaves takes place in:
(a) Grana of chloroplast
(b) Stroma of chloroplast
(c) The nucleus of palisade cells
(d) The cytoplasm of palisade cells
Answer: (a) Grana of chloroplast

(vii) An example of a biodegradable substance is:
(a) Aluminum
(b) Paper
(c) Plastic
(d) Steel
Answer: (b) Paper

(viii) The part that is cut in Vasectomy is:
(a) Urethra
(b) Oviduct
(c) Fallopian tube
(d) Vas deferens
Answer: (d) Vas deferens

(ix) The gestation period of a human fetus is:
(a) 40 days
(b) 280 days
(c) 280 weeks
(d) 40 months
Answer: (b) 280 days

(x) The part of the human eye where the rods and cones are located is:
(a) Iris
(b) Retina
(c) Sclera

(d) Choroid
Answer : (b) Retina

(xi) Organ of Corti is present in:
(a) Utriculus
(b) Sacculus
(c) Cochlea
(d) Incus
Answer: (c) Cochlea

(xii) The outermost covering of the brain is:
(a) Arachnoid
(b) Pia mater
(c) Pericardium
(d) Dura mater
Answer : (d) Dura mater

(xiii) Cytokinins are predominantly present in:
(a) Meristematic tissues
(b) Permanent tissues
(c) Endodermis
(d) Epidermis
Answer : (a) Meristematic tissues

(xiv) Marine fish when placed in tap water bursts because of:
(a) Diffusion
(b) Plasmolysis
(c) Endosmosis
(d) Exosmosis
Answer: (c) Endosmosis

(xv) Urine is carried from the kidney to the urinary bladder by:
(a) Uterus
(b) Urethra
(c) Umbilical cord
(d) Ureter
Answer: (d) Ureter

Question 2.

(i) Name the following: **[5]**
(a) The suppressed allele of a gene.
(b) The knot-like mass of blood capillaries in Bowman's capsule.

(c) The mineral element required for the synthesis of thyroxine.

(d) One gaseous compound that depletes the ozone layer.

(e) The statistical study of the human population.

Answer:

(a) Recessive allele

(b) Glomerulus

(c) Iodine

(d) CFCs

(e) Demography

(ii) Arrange and rewrite the terms in each group in the correct order to be in a logical sequence beginning with the term that is underlined. **[5]**

Soil water, Xylem, Root hair, Cortex

(a) Tympanum, Incus, Malleus, Stapes

(b) Pulmonary Vein, Left Ventricle, Aorta, Left auricle

(c) Sperm, Urethra, Sperm duct, Epididymis

(d) Aqueous humor, Optic nerve, Retina, Lens

Answer:

(a) Soil water, Root hair, Cortex, Xylem

(b) Tympanum, Malleus, Incus, Stapes

(c) Pulmonary Vein, Left auricle, Left Ventricle, Aorta

(d) Sperm, Epididymis, Sperm duct, Urethra

(e) Aqueous humor, Lens, Retina, Optic nerve

(iii) Match the items given in Column I with the most appropriate ones in Column II and rewrite the correct matching pairs. **[5]**

Answer:

Column I	Column II
(a) Natality	1. DDT
(b) Soil pollutant	2. Death rate
(c) Starch test	3. Carbon monoxide
(d) Mortality	4. Lodine solution
(e) Air pollutant	5. Lime solution
	6. Birth rate
	7. Growth rate

(a) Birth rate

(b) DDT

(c) Iodine solution

(d) Death rate

(e) Carbon monoxide

(iv) Choose the odd one out from the following terms and name the category to which the others belong: **[5]**

(a) The thyroid gland, Lacrimal gland, Pituitary gland, and Adrenal gland.

(b) Detergents, Sewage, X-rays, Oil spills

(c) The spinal cord, Cerebrum, Pons, Cerebellum

(d) Chloroplast, Cell wall, Large Vacuoles, Centrosome.

(e) Auxin, Oxytocin, Gibberellin, Cytokinin

Answer:

(a) Lacrimal gland - Endocrine Gland

(b) X-rays - Water Pollution

(c) Spinal cord - Brain

(d) Centrosome - Plant Cell

(e) Oxytocin - Plant Hormones

(v) State the exact location of the following structures: **[5]**

(a) Thylakoids

(b) Corpus callosum

(c) Chordae tendency

(d) Prostate gland

(e) Adrenal glands

Answer:

(a) each granum of the chloroplast

(b) A thick band of nerve fibers joining two cerebral hemispheres

(c) Arises from the muscular projections of the vertical walls known as papilla muscles in b/w right atrioventricular valve

(d) Present at the base of the urinary bladder surrounding the urethra

(e) Situated at the top of each kidney and are enclosed in a connective tissue capsule.

Section B

(Attempt any four questions from this Section.)

Question 3.

(i) Define Guttation. **[1]**

(ii) Give one difference between Lenticels and Stomata. **[2]**

(iii) What is Parthenocarpy? Give one example. **[2]**

(iv) State Mendel's Law of Segregation. **[2]**

(v) Study the diagram given below and answer the questions that follow: **[3]**

(a) Name the process being studied in the above experiment.

(b) What will you observe with regard to the level of water when this setup is placed in bright sunlight?

(c) Mention one adaptation found in plants to overcome the process mentioned in (i).

Answer:

(i) Guttation is the process of secretion of water droplets from the pores of some vascular plants like grass. Guttation is often confused with dew droplets that condense from the atmosphere onto the plant's surface.

(ii) The main difference between stomata and lenticels is that stomata mainly occur in the lower epidermis of leaves, whereas lenticels occur in the periderm of the woody trunk or stems.

(iii) Parthenocarpy, development of fruit without fertilization. The fruit resembles a normally produced fruit but is seedless. Ex. Pineapple

(iv) Mendel's law of segregation states that: "During the formation of gamete, each gene separates from each other so that each gamete carries only one allele for each gene." The Law of segregation is the second law of inheritance.

(v) **(a)** Transpirations

(b) The level of water will power which indicates loss of water by the shoot d to transpiration because due to oil on the surface, and no water loss due to evaporation.

(c) Sunken stomata and narrow leaves in Nerium

Question 4.

(i) Expand the abbreviation - A T P. **[1]**

(ii) Name any two nitrogenous bases. **[2]**

(iii) The addition of salt to pickles prevents the growth of bacteria. Explain by giving two suitable reasons. **[2]**

(iv) Mention two adaptations in leaves to perform Photosynthesis. **[2]**

(v) Given below is a diagram representing a stage during mitotic cell division. **[3]**

Answer the following questions:

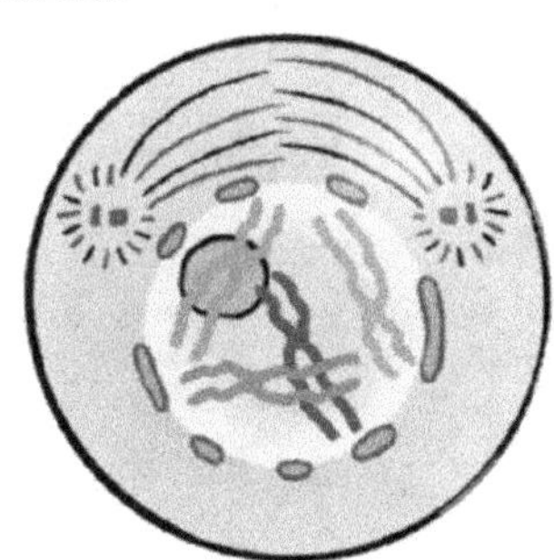

(a) Identify the stage.

(b) Give a suitable reason for your answer in (a).

(c) Name the stage that follows the one shown in the diagram.

Answer:

(i) Adenosine triphosphate

(ii) Adenine (A), thymine (T), cytosine (C), and guanine (G).

(iii) The addition of salt to pickles prevents the growth of bacteria because they turn flaccid.
Reason: The addition of salt to pickles increases the concentration and when bacterias come in contact it undergoes exosmosis and thus becomes flaccid or plasmolyzed leading to their death.

(iv) **(a)** Large surface area for maximum light absorption.
(b) Leaf arrangement at a right angle to a light source.

(v) **(a)** Early prophase.
(b) Centriole moving apart, chromosome becomes a distinct, spindle fiber appear.
(c) After the late prophase, the next stage is Metaphase.

Question 5.

(i) Define - Excretion. **[1]**

(ii) What is the significance of the Hepatic Portal Vein? **[2]**

(iii) State two functions of vitreous humor. **[2]**

(iv) Which gland secretes Glucagon? What is its effect on blood sugar levels? **[2]**

(v) Draw a neat labeled diagram to show the internal structure of a human kidney. **[3]**

Answer:

(i) Excretion is a process in which metabolic waste is eliminated from an organism. In vertebrates, this is primarily carried out by the lungs, kidneys, and skin. This is in contrast with secretion, where the substance may have specific tasks after leaving the cell.

(ii) Significance of Hepatic Portal Vein:
(a) The hepatic portal vein carries 75% of the hepatic blood flow and hence is crucial. It is not a true vein as it does not conduct blood directly to the heart.
(b) It supplies veins with metabolic substrates.

(iii) **(a)** It helps in keeping the shape of the eyeball.
(b) It protects the retina and its nerve ending.

(iv) Glucagon is secreted by the alpha cells in the pancreas. It raises the sugar level in the blood because it stimulates the breakdown of glycogen of glucose in the liver.

(v)

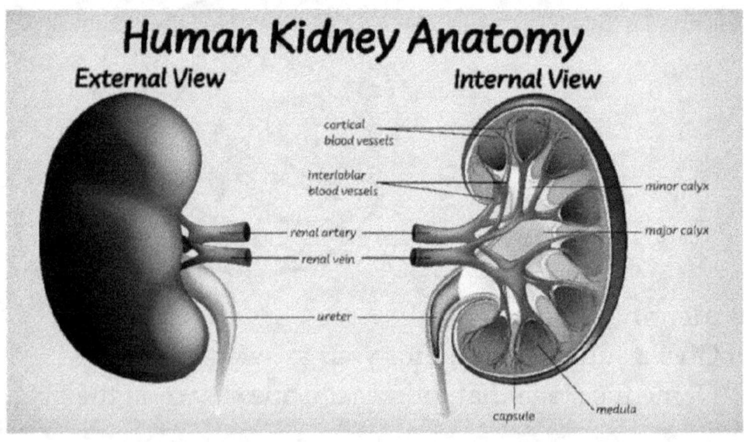

Question 6.

(i) Define - Gene. **[1]**

(ii) Differentiate between Cell wall and Cell membrane with reference to permeability. **[2]**

(iii) State the function of Medulla Oblongata with a suitable example. **[2]**

(iv) Color blindness is generally seen in males. Explain. **[2]**

(v) Study the diagram given below and answer the questions that follow: **[3]**

(a) Identify the structure.

(b) In which part of the ear is it located?

(c) What is the function of the part marked A?

Answer:

(i) A gene is a basic unit of heredity and a sequence of nucleotides in DNA that encodes the synthesis of a gene product, either RNA or protein.

(ii) Cell wall is thin and permeable
Cell membrane is very thin and semi-permeable

(iii) To control the activities of internal organs like the beating of the heart and many other involuntary actions.

(iv) It's passed down on the X chromosome, and red-green color blindness is more common in men. This is because: Males have only 1X chromosomes, from their mothers. If that X chromosome has the gene for red-green color blindness (instead of a normal X chromosome), they will have red-green color blindness.

(v) **(a)** Part of the human ear.

(b) Inner Part

(c) Semicircular canals- Response to the change in position, ex. it is concerned with the sense of dynamic balance.

Question 7.

(i) Explain - Accommodation of eye. **[1]**

(ii) Give two reasons for a sharp rise in the world's human population. **[2]**

(iii) Mention two functions of Amniotic fluid. **[2]**

(iv) What is the difference between Phenotype and Genotype? **[2]**

(v) Draw neat labeled diagrams showing the cross sections of an Artery and a Vein. **[3]**

Answer:

(i) The process of focusing the eye to see an object at a different distance is called Accommodation.

(ii) **(a)** Industrial Revolution

(b) New discovery in medical science

(iii) **(a)** Protects the embryo from physical damage.

(b) Allow the fetus some restricted movement

(iv) Difference between Phenotype and Genotype:

Genotype	Phenotype
The hereditary information of the organism is in the form of a gene in the DNA and remains the same throughout life.	The characters of an area are known as phenotypes.
The same genotype produces the same phenotype.	The same phenotype may or may not belong to the same genotype.
Present inside the body as genetic material	Expression of genes as the external appearance
The genotype is inherited from the parent to the offspring	The phenotype is not inherited from the parent

(v)

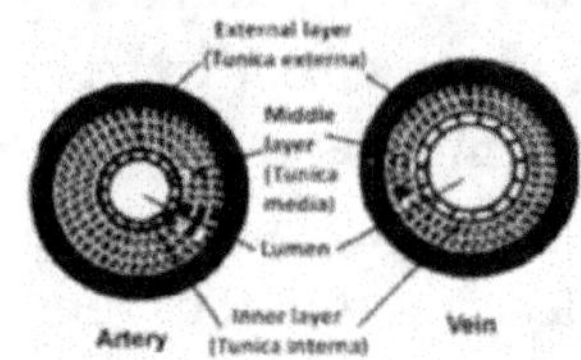

Question 8.

(i) Define - Pollution. **[1]**

(ii) Plants droop on a hot day even though the soil is well watered. Explain. **[2]**

(iii) Differentiate between Menarche and Menopause. **[2]**

(iv) State two harmful effects of acid rain. **2]**

(v) The diagram given below shows a type of tropism. Answer the questions that follow: **[3]**

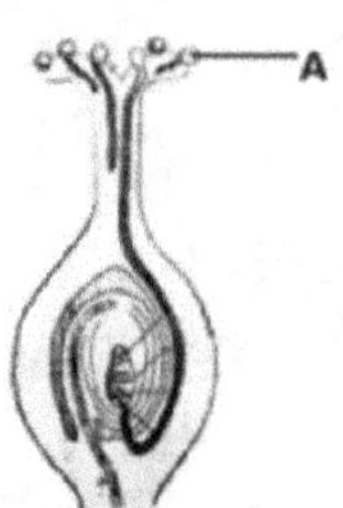

(a) Name the type of tropism.

(b) Define the above-mentioned tropism.

(c) Give an example of a stimulant that helps in the growth of the part marked

Answer:

(i) Pollution is the introduction of harmful materials into the environment. These harmful materials are called pollutants. Pollutants can be natural, such as volcanic ash.

(ii) On a hot day, herbaceous plants wilt even in well-watered soil because their rate of transpiration exceeds the rate of water absorption by the roots. Due to less water in the cells, they become flaccid, and leaves become soft and wilt.

(iii) Menarche is the first menstruation of the human female on the attainment of puberty that occurs at about 13 years of age, whereas menopause is the phase in the human female's life when ovulation and menstruation stop that occurs at about 45-55 years of age.

(iv) Dead or dying trees are a common sight in areas affected by acid rain. Acid rain leaches aluminum from the soil. That aluminum may be harmful to plants as well as animals. Acid rain also removes minerals and nutrients from the soil that trees need to grow.

(v)

(a) Chemotropism

(b) Due to chemicals

(c) A is pollen grain and a stimulant is Auxin

ICSE 2023 EXAMINATION

SAMPLE TEST PAPER-1

BIOLOGY

(SCIENCE PAPER-2)

Maximum Marks: 80

Time allowed: Two hours

Answers to this Paper must be written on the paper provided separately.

You will not be allowed to write during first 15 minutes.

This time is to be spent in reading the question paper.

The time given at the head of this Paper is the time allowed for writing the answers.

(Section A is compulsory. Attempt any four questions from Section B.
The intended marks for questions or parts of questions are given in brackets [ ].

Section A

Answer all the questions from this section

Question 1.

Name the following by choosing the correct answers to the questions from the given options. (Do not copy the question, Write the correct answer only.) **[15]**

(i) Leucocytes are white blood corpuscles. Functions of leucocytes are:

(a) Phagocytosis and inflammation

(b) Formation of antibodies

(c) Transport

(d) Both (a) and (b)

Answer. (d) Both (a) and (b)

Explanation: Leucocytes are white blood cells involved in body defence. Functions of leucocytes are phagocytosis. inflammation, and formation of antibodies.

(ii) Thirst, sweat and hunger are controlled by:

(a) Hypothalamus

(b) Cerebrum

(c) Mid brain

(d) Medulla

Answer. (a) Hypothalamus

Explanation:

Hypothalamus is a part of the (Fore brain). It controls the hormonal secretions from endocrine glands. Hormone secreted from posterior pituitary gland are released through it. This is the centre of hunger, thirst, body temperature control, love, hate etc. Blood pressure, metabolism of water, sweat, anger, joy etc. are controlled by it.

(iii) Sclera is covered by a thin transparent membrane called

(a) Retina

(b) Ciliary muscle

(c) Iris

(d) Conjunctiva

Answer. (d) Conjunctiva

Explanation:

Near the front of the eye, in the area protected by the eyelids, the sclera is covered by a thin, transparent membrane (conjunctiva), which runs to the edge of the comea. The conjunctiva also covers the moist back surface of the eyelids and eyeballs.

(iv) Coordination and control of reflex actions is function of:

(a) Pons

(b) Medulla

(c) Brain

(d) Spinal cord

Answer. (d) Spinal cord

(v) Ultrafiltration occurs in:

(a) Bowman's capsule

(b) Proximal convoluted tubule

(c) Henle's loop

(d) Distal convoluted tubule

Answer. (a) Bowman's capsule

Explanation:

Ultrafiltration is one of the majorstep for the formation of urine. Blood flows through Bowman's capsule under great pressure. This happens because efferent (outgoing) arteriole is narrower than afferent (incoming) arteriole. This high pressure causes liquid part of blood to filter out from glomerulus into renal tubule. This process is called ultrafiltration.

(vi) pH of normal urine is:

(a) 4.5 to 7

(b) 3 to 8

(c) 5 to 8

(d) 7 to 8

Answer. (c) 5 to 8

Explanation:

The pH of normal urine is 5 to 8 .

(vii) Cranial nerves:

(a) Consist of 12 pairs of nerves

(b) Found at dorsal surface of the brain

(c) It carries information from spinal nerve to other body part

(d) It is part of central nervous system

Answer. (a) Consist of 12 pairs of nerves

Explanation:

Cranial nerve is the nerve which exit from the cranium of the brain. Cranial nerve are 12 pairs of nerves which are found on the ventral (bottom) surface of the brain. Cranial nerves relay information between the brain and part of the body, primarily to and from regions of the head and neck. It is part of Peripheral nervous system.

(viii) The main function of pancreas as andocrine gland in human body:

(a) Help in digestive system

(b) Regulate blood sugar levels

(c) Regulate the iron concentration

(d) Control other hormones

Answer. (b) Regulate blood sugar levels

Explanation:

Regulate the blood sugar level is main function of pancreas as an endocrine gland in human body. Pancreas is both an endocrine gland as well as exocrine gland. It secretes 3 hormones, that is,Insulin: Checks rise of sugar level in blood.

Glucagon: Stimulates breakdown of glycogen in liver to gluonse, thereby raising sugar levels. Somatostatin: Regulatory hormone which inhibits secretion of insulin and glucagon.

(ix) In Human brain memory power is found in:

(a) Medulla oblongata

(b) Thalamus

(c) Cerebrum

(d) Cerebellum

Answer. (b) Cerebrum

Explanation:

Cerebrum is the largest part of fore brain. It is the most developed part of the brain. Cerebrum acts as the centre of wisdom, memory, will power, movements, knowledge and thinking. It also functions as the analysis and cordination of muscular movement received from sensory organs.

(x) Jelly-like fluid present in the eye called:

(a) Pupil

(b) Posterior chamber

(c) Vitreous humor

(d) Retina.

Answer. (c) Vitreous humor

Explanation:

The back section (posterior segment) extends from the back surface of the lens to the retina. It contains a jellylike fluid called the vitreous humour.

(xi) Which of the following is not an excretory organ in human?

(a) Lungs
(b) Kidney
(c) Mouth
(d) Sweat glands.
Answer. (c) Mouth
Explanation:
Excretion in humans is done through sweat glands, lungs, kidney organs. Mouth is not an excretory organ.

(xii) Organ of Balancing of sound is:
(a) Peripheral vestibular system
(b) Acoustic meatus
(c) Tympanic membrane
(d) Eustachian tube
Answer. (a) Peripheral vestibular system
Explanation:
The peripheral vestibular system is organ of balance. The peripheral vestibular system is responsible for maintaining balance, coordinating the position of the head and eye movement. The system consists of sacs filled with endolymph, with the fibres of the vestibulocochlear nerve distributed on the walls of these sacs.

(xiii) White blood cells are also called:
(a) Erythrocytes
(b) Leukocytes
(c) Thrombocytes
(d) Monocytes
Answer. (b) Leukocytes
Explanation:
White blood cells are also called leukocytes because leuko means white. WBCs contain nucleus but do not contain haemoglobin.

(xiv) Natural Reflex is:
(a) Voluntary reflex
(b) Experimental reflex
(c) It is Inborn reflex
(d) Differs in different individuals
Answer. (c) It is Inborn reflex
Explanation:
It is one in which no previous experience or learning is acquired. This is inborn reflex. Examp Blinking, coughing, sneezing, swallowing.

(xv) When lens of eye becomes foggy it cause:

(a) Astigmatism
(b) Glaucoma
(c) Cataract
(d) Amblyopia

Answer. (c) Cataract

Explanation:

A cataract develops when the lens in your eye, which is normally clear, becomes foggy. For your eye to see, light passes through a clear lens. The lens is behind your iris. The lens focuses the light so that your brain and eye can work together to process information into a picture. When a cataract clouds over the lens, your eye can't focus light in the same way. This leads to blurry vision or other vision loss (trouble seeing).

Question 2.

(i) Name the following: **[5]**

(a) The mineral element essential for the clotting of blood.
(b) The cells of the testes that produce male hormones.
(c) The nutritive layer of the eye which also prevents reflection of light.
(d) The structural and functional unit of the kidney.
(e) The part of the chloroplast where the light reaction of photosynthesis takes place.

Answer.

(a) Calcium
(b) Interstitial cells/Leydig cells
(c) Choroid
(d) Nephron/Uriniferous tubule
(e) Thylakoids

(ii) Given below are sets of five terms each. Rewrite the terms in correct order in a logical sequence beginning with the first word that is underlined: **[5]**

(a) Stimulus, Response, Receptor, Effector, Spinal cord.
(b) Root hair, Endodermis, Epidermis, Xylem, Cortex.
(c) Conjunctiva, Yellow spot, Pupil, Vitreous Humour, Aqueous Humour.
(d) Sperm, Urethra, sperm duct, epididymis,
(e) Artery, Capillaries, Venule, Vein, Arteriole.

Answer.

(a) Stimulus, receptor, spinal cord, effector, response
(b) Root hair, epidermis, cortex, endodermis, xylem
(c) Conjunctiva, aqueous humour, pupil, vitreous humour, yellow spot
(d) Sperm, sperm duct, epididymis, Urethra.
(e) Artery, arteriole, capillaries, venule, vein.

(iii) Match the items in Column I with that which is most appropriate in Column II. **[5]**

Column I	Column II

(a)	Pacemaker	i	Associated with static body balance
(b)	Stroma	ii	Chordae tendinae
(c)	Afferent nerve	iii	Site of light reaction
(d)	Prolactin	iv	Motor neuron
(e)	Saccules	v	S A node
		vi	Stimulates production of milk by the mammary gland
		vii	Site of dark reaction
		viii	Transmits impulses from receptor organ to spinal cord

Answer.

Column I	Column II
(1) Pacemaker	(e) SA node
(2) Stroma	(g) Site of dark reaction
(3) Afferent nerve	(h) Transmists impulses from receptor organ to spinal cord
(4) Prolactin	(f) Stimulates production of milk by the mammary gland
(5) Saccules	(a) Associated with static body balance

(iv) Given below are six sets with four terms each. In each set one term is odd and cannot be grouped in the same category to which the other three belong. Identify the odd one in each set and name the category to which the remaining three belong. The first one has been done as an example. **[5]**

Example: Calyx, Corolla, Stamens, Midrib

Odd term: Midrib

(a) Hemoglobin, Glucagon, Iodopsin, Rhodopsin.

(b) Urethra, Uterus, Urinary bladder, Ureter.

(c) Transpiration, Photosynthesis, Phagocytosis, Guttation.

(d) Cyton, Photon, Axon, Dendron.

(e) Oxytocin, Insulin, Prolactin, Progesterone.

Answer.

(a) Odd: Glucagon

(b) Odd : Uterus

(c) Odd: Phagocytosis

(d) Odd: Photon

(e) Odd: Insulin

(v) Give the exact location of the following: **[5]**

(a) Lenticels

(b) Prostate gland

(c) Thyroid gland

(d) Centrosome

(e) Mitral valve.

Answer.

(a) Lenticels: Loose aggregration of cells in the bark of the stems and roots of certain plants for gaseous exchange.

(b) Prostate gland: At the base of urinary bladder.

(c) Thyroid gland: In the neck region at the base of larynx.

(d) Centrosome: Situated close to the nucleus in Eukaryotic cell.

(e) Mitral valve or bicuspid valve: Present in the left atrio-ventricular aperture within the heart.

Section B

(Attempt any four questions from this Section.)

Question 3.

(i) Define transpiration **[1]**

Answer. Transpiration is the loss of water in the form of water vapours from the leaves and other aerial parts of the plant.

(ii) Differentiate between the following pairs on the basis of what is mentioned within brackets: Photolysis and Photophosphorylation. (Definition) **[2]**

Answer.

Photolysis	Photophosphorylation
Thelightenergyabsorbed	The energy rich
by chlorophyll splits	electrons released
water into hydrogen and	during photolysis of
oxygen and releases two	water are used in the
electrons.	synthesis of ATP from
	ADP.

(iii) What is Reflex action? Explain it. **[2]**

Answer. A reflex action is a nerve mediated spontaneous, automatic, involuntary response to a stimulus acting on a specific receptor. The route of every reflex passes through an aggregation of nervous tissue, either brain or spinal cord. Brain or spinal cord aids in transfer of sensory stimulus to motor response.

(iv) State Mendel's law of Dominance. **[2]**

Answer. Mendel's Law of Dominance : Out of a pair of contrasting characters present together in an offspring, one dominates over the other or one character is expressed while other remains suppressed

(v) The figure given below represents an experiment to demonstrate a particular aspect of photosynthesis. The alphabet '**A**' represents a certain condition inside the flask.

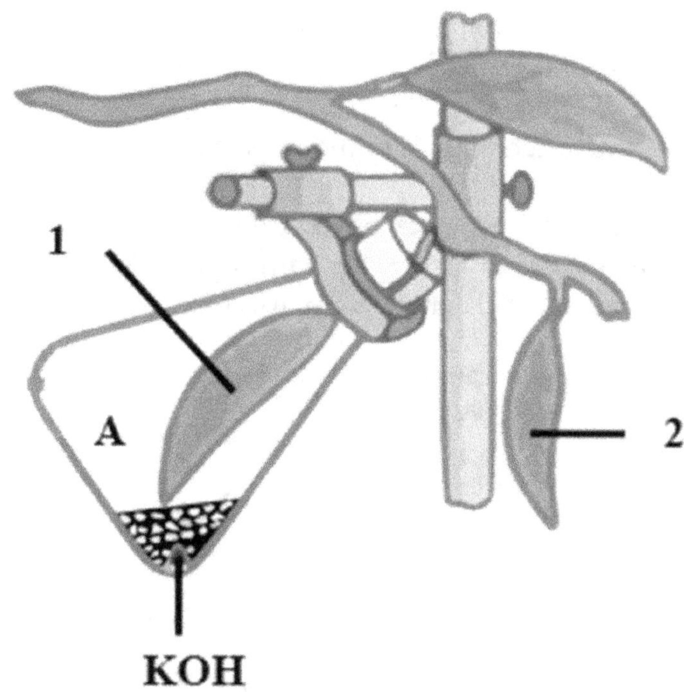

(a) What is the aim of the experiment?
(b) Identify the special condition inside the flask.
(c) Name an alternative chemical that can be used instead of KOH.
(d) In what manner do the leaves 1 and 2 differ at the end of the starch test?

Answer.

(a) Aim was to prove that CO_2 is necessary for photosynthesis.
(b) NOCO_2 in the flask.
(c) CaO (limestone), potassium pyrogallate.
(d) Leaf 1 will turn brown indicating absence of starch.
Leaf 2 will turn blue-black at the end of starch test indicating presence of starch.

Question 4.

(i) Expand the biological abbreviations. ABA **[1]**
Answer: Abscisic acid .

(ii) Name the two type of cell divisions **[2]**
Answer. Mitosis and meiosis

(iii) The human eye adapts itself to bright light and dim light. Explain? **[2]**
Answer. When we move from a brightly lighted area to a dark room i.e., in dim light, we experience difficulty in seeing objects for some time. Slowly, our vision is improved. This is called dark adaptation. The pupil dilates to allow more light to enter the eyes and rhodopsin/visual purple is generated.
When we enter a brightly lighted area after being in a dimly lighted area for a period of time, we experience a dazzling light for short period after which our vision improves. This is called

the light adaptation. Pupil constricts to allow less light to mentionur eyes and rhodopsin pigment is degenerate.

(iv) Mention any three adaptations found in plants to overcome the process of transpiration?

Answer. **[2]**

(a) The number of stomata may be reduced.

(b) Leaves may become narrow as modification of leaves into spines.

(c) A thick layer of cuticle on the leaf surface helps to decrease transpiration.

(v) Study the following diagram carefully and then answer the questions that follow. The diagram is depicting a defect of the human eye: **[3]**

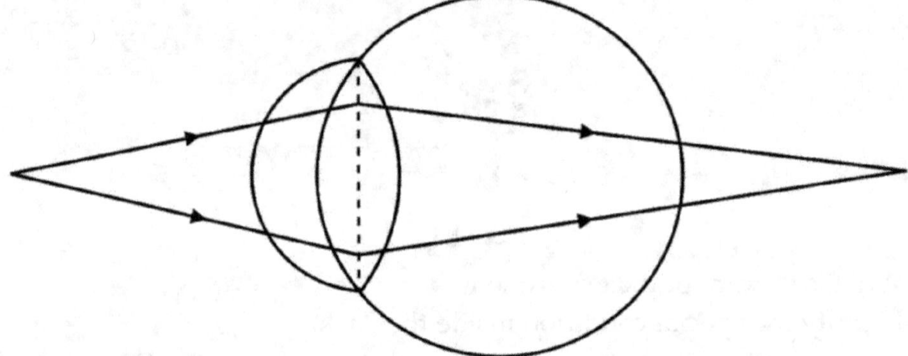

(a) Identify the defect shown in the diagram.

(b) Give two possible reasons for the above defect.

(c) Draw a neat labelled diagram to show how the above defect can be rectified.

Answer. Far sightness or hypermetropia.

(a) Lens is flattened or less convex.

(b) Eyeball is short from front to back.

(c)

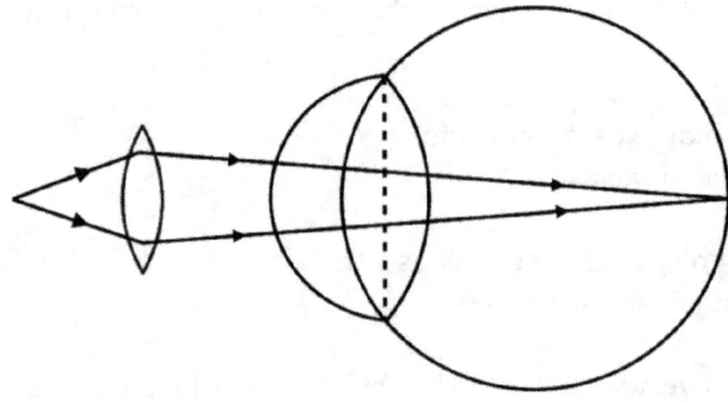

Question 5.

(i) Define Cytokinesis in plant cells? **[1]**

Answer. Process in which the cytoplasmic content of the cell is divided into two new daughter cells by formation of a cell plate which extends from centre to periphery of the cell is called cytokinesis.

(ii) What is the significance of photosynthesis in plant? **[2]**
Answer. The significance of photosynthesis process is that it is the only biological process which releases oxygen into the atmosphere that supports all life forms on the earth's surface. Green plants synthesize their food by photosynthesis. All organisms are directly or indirectly dependent on green plants for their food.

(iii) State the function of thrombocytes **[2]**
Answer. Thrombocytes help in clotting of blood.

(iv) The left ventricle of the heart has a thicker wall than the right ventricle. **[2]**
Answer. The left ventricle pumps blood to the farthest points of the body like toes, feet, brain and other parts of the body whereas right ventricle pumps blood only up to the lungs. So walls of the left ventricle are thicker than the walls of right ventricle.

(v) Draw neat and labelled diagrams of Malpighian Capsule. **[3]**
Answer.

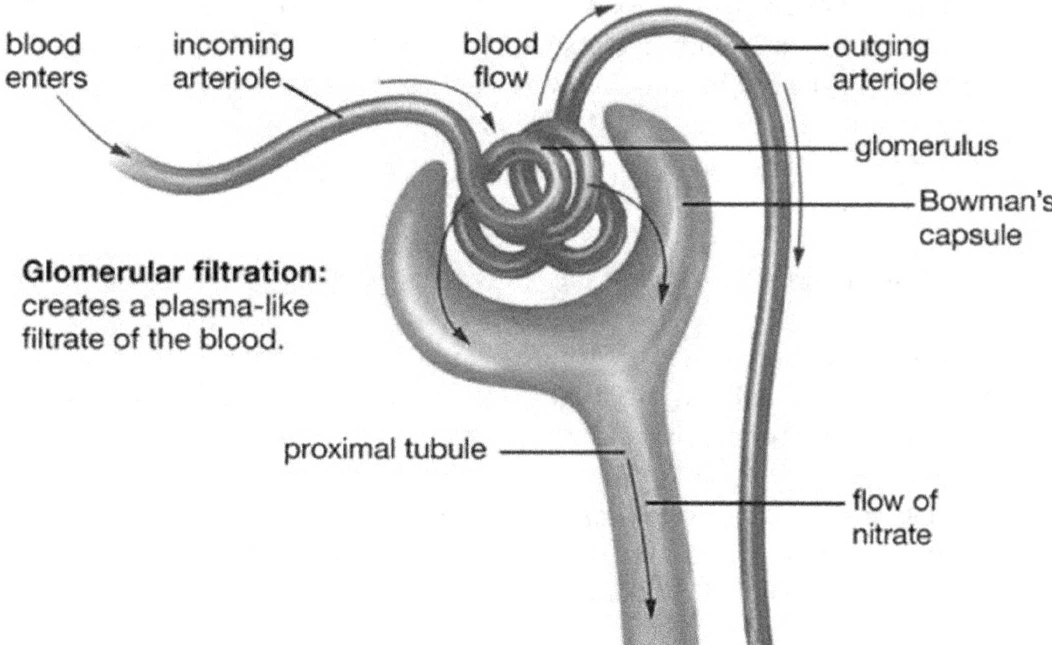

Question 6.

(i) Define - Excretion. **[1]**

Answer Excretion is a process in which metabolic waste is eliminated from an organism. In vertebrates, this is primarily carried out by the lungs, kidneys, and skin. This is in contrast with secretion, where the substance may have specific tasks after leaving the cell.

(ii) Difference between Mitral value and semilunar value. **[2]**

Mitral Value	Semilunar Value
(a) Located between left auricle and left Ventricle **(b)** Regulates the flow of blood from left atrium to left ventrivcle and prevents its backflow.	Located at the bases of aorta and pulmonary artery. These are also located in the veins and lymph vessels. Prevents backflow of blood from aorta and pulmonary artery into ventricles. It also has same function in veins and lymph vessels.

(iii) Give two main functions of the kidney. Describe the process how these functions are performed by the kidneys. **[2]**

Answer. The two main functions of the kidney are:

(a) Urea excretion. It is done by the nephrons which reabsorb all the useful products from the ultrafiltrate of the glomeruli but do not absorb urea.

(b) Osmoregulation. The water content of the ultrafiltrate is mostly reabsorbed but extra water is allowed to be excreted along with urine. The amount of water in the urine is controlled by ADH. More ADH means more reabsorption and less ADH means less reabsorption and, therefore, excretion of more water. The two functions of kidneys are performed by the combination of three processes:

i. Filtration

ii. Reabsorption

iii. Secretion.

(iv) Give How do kidneys maintain the water balance when water content in the body is mgn or low? **[2]**

Answer. Kidneys excrete more dilute urine when the water content is more in the body tissues and blood and excrete more concentrated urine when water is les. Thus, kidneys maintain a water balance in our body.

(v) The diagram given alongside represents a layer of epidermal cells showing a full-grown root hair. Study the diagram and answer the questions that follow: **[3]**

(a) Name the parts labelled A, B, C and D.

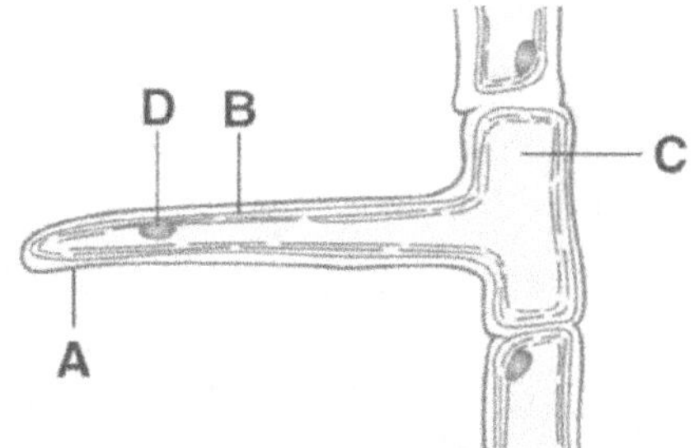

(b) The root hair cell is in a turgid state. Name and explain the process that caused this state.

(c) Mention one distinct difference between the parts labelled A and B.

(d) Draw a diagram of the above root hair cell as it would appear when a concentrated solution of fertilizers is added near it.

Answer.

(a) A-Cell wall, B-Cell membrane, C-Cytoplasm, D-Nucleus.

(b) It is due to endosmosis because the cell sap of root hair is more concentrated than the surrounding water in soil.

(c) The cell wall of root coll is rigid and permeable to all minerals and water Whereas cell membrane is flexible and selectively permeable to certain mineral.

(d)

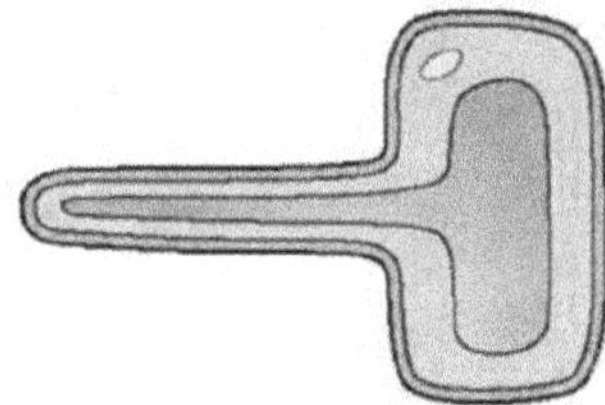

Question 7.

(i) What is cell body or cyton ? **[1]**

Answer: The cell body or cyton, which consists of a nucleus and the other organelles, generally found in eukaryotic cells.

(ii) Why is it not possible to demonstrate respiration in a green plant kept in sunlight? [2]

Answer. When a plant is kept in sunlight, CO_2 released by respiration gets used bt photosysnthesis to synthesise food. So, no carbon dioxide is liberated, and respiration cannot be demonstrated.

(iii) Why do xerophytes have their leaves reduced or modified to form spines? [2]

Answer. Xerophytes grow in areas where there is scarcity of water in soil and air. Xerophytes reduce the surface area by forming spines or reduction in size (20%) to reduce transpiration and conserve water.

(iv) Difference between cuticular transpiration and lenticular transpiration? [2]

Answer:

Cuticular Transpiration	Lenticular Transpiration
It takes place through the thin cuticle covering the leaves of the plant.	It takes place through the openings on the stems of woody plants, called lenticels.

Study the diagram given below and then answer the questions that follow: **[3]**

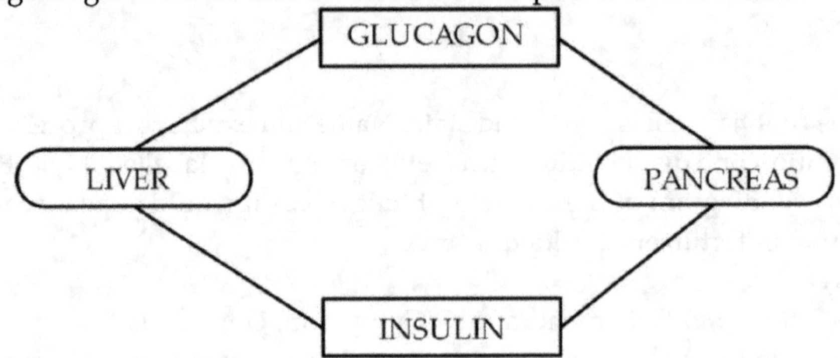

(a) Name the cells of the pancreas that produce (1) glucagon (2) insulin.
(b) State the main function of (1) glucagon (2) insulin.
(c) Why is the pancreas referred to as an exo-endocrine gland?
(d) Why is insulin not given orally but is injected into the body?
(e) What is the technical term for the cells of the pancreas that produce endocrine hormones?
(f) Where in the body is the pancreas located?

Answer.

(a) (1) Beta cells
(2) Alpha cells

(b) (1) Glucagon raises the blood glucose level.
(2) Insulin lowers the blood glucose level.

(c) Pancreas produces insulin and glucagon and hence, serve as an endocrine gland. In addition, it also releases pancreatic juice via the pancreatic duct to duodenum hence, serve as an exocrine gland.

(d) Insulin is not taken orally because, like all other proteins introduced into the gastrointestinal tract, will break into small fragments and its activity will be lost.

(e) Islet of Langerhans

(f) It is located posterior and inferior to the stomach, inside the loop of duodenum.

Question 8.

(i) Define stomata?

Answer These are located on the lower surface of dicot leaves and both upper and lower surfaces of monocot leaves. **[1]**

These lose water vapor which is termed stomatal transpiration.

(ii) Why do herbaceous plants show wilting of leaves during mid-day but recover in the evening? **[2]**

Answer. The rate of transpiration is maximum during the mid-day. Large amount of water is lost compared to the intake hence, the leaves become flaccid and show wilting. In the evening, the rate of transpiration is reduced and the uptake of water is balanced by the necessary amount in the leaves, therefore, they recover.

(iii) Name the blood vessel entering the kidney and the one leaving it. Give three differences in the composition of the blood in these two blood vessels. **[2]**

Answer. Renal artery enters the kidney and renal vein leaves the kidney for the blood flow.

Renal Vein	Renal Artery
(a) Has less Urea.	Has more urea.
(b) Has less oxygen.	Has more oxygen.
(c) Has more carbon dioxide.	Has less carbon dioxide.

(iv) Give two examples of reflex actions in our daily leu. **[2]**

Answer. (i) Application of brakes of a bicycle, scooter or a car while driving.

(ii) Withdrawal of hand when it touches a hot object or live electric wire.

(v) Study the diagram given below and answer the questions that follow: **[3]**

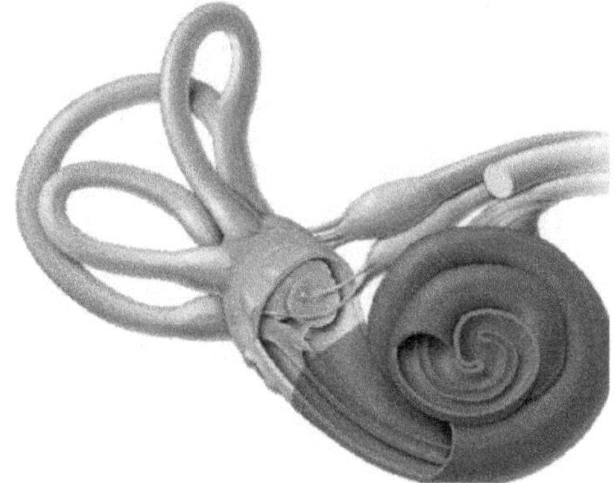

(a) Identify the structure.

(b) In which part of the ear is it located?

(c) What is the function of the part marked A?

Answer

(a) Part of the human ear.

(b) Inner Part

(c) Semicircular canals- Response to the change in position, ex. it is concerned with the sense of dynamic balance.

ICSE 2023 EXAMINATION

SAMPLE TEST PAPER-2

BIOLOGY

(SCIENCE PAPER-2)

Maximum Marks: 80

Time allowed: Two hours

Answers to this Paper must be written on the paper provided separately.

You will not be allowed to write during first 15 minutes.

This time is to be spent in reading the question paper.

The time given at the head of this Paper is the time allowed for writing the answers.

(Section A is compulsory. Attempt any four questions from Section B.

The intended marks for questions or parts of questions are given in brackets [ ].

Section A

Answer all the questions from this section

Question 1

Choose the Correct Option **[15]**

(i) Which of the following is not an excretory organ in human?

(a) Lungs

(b) Kidney

(c) Mouth

(d) Sweat glands.

Answer. (c) Mouth

Explanation:

Excretion in humans is done through sweat glands, lungs, kidney organs. Mouth is not an excretory organ.

(ii) Organ of Balancing of sound is:

(a) Tympanic membrane

(b) Peripheral vestibular system

(c) Eustachian tube

(d) Acoustic meatus

Answer. (b) Peripheral vestibular system

Explanation:

The peripheral vestibular system is organ of balance. The peripheral vestibular system is responsible for maintaining balance, coordinating the position of the head and eye movement. The system consists of sacs filled with endolymph, with the fibres of the vestibulocochlear nerve distributed on the walls of these sacs.

(iii) White blood cells are also called:

(a) Erythrocytes

(b) Leukocytes

(c) Thrombocytes

(d) Monocytes
Answer. (b) Leukocytes
Explanation:
White blood cells are also called leukocytes because leucon means white. WBCs contain nucleus but do not contain hemoglobin.

(iv) Natural Reflex is:
(a) Inborn reflex
(b) Voluntary reflex
(c) Differs in different individuals
(d) Experimental reflex
Answer. (a) It is Inborn reflex
Explanation:
It is one in which no previous experience or learning is acquired. This is inborn reflex. Example Blinking, coughing, sneezing, swallowing.

(v) When lens of eye becomes foggy it causes:
(a) Cataract
(b) Astigmatism
(c) Amblyopia
(d) Glaucoma
Answer. (a) Cataract
Explanation:
A cataract develops when the lens in your eye, which is normally clear, becomes foggy. For your eye to see, light passes through a clear lens. The lens is behind your iris. The lens focuses the light so that your brain and eye can work together to process information into a picture. When a cataract clouds over the lens, your eye can't focus light in the same way. This leads to blurry vision or other vision loss (trouble seeing),

(vi) Which hormone promote the release of carbohydrate, fats and protein in human body?
(a) Androgen
(b) Calcitonin
(c) Thymopoietin
(d) Cortisol
Answer. (d) Cortisol
Explanation:
Cortisol hormone controls the metabolism of carbohydrate, fat and protein in the blood. It promotes the glycogenesis in the liver. It helps in maintain blood pressure and blood glucose (sugar) level.

(vii) The range of blood platelets count in normal adult is:
(a) 250,000 to 400,000percu. mm

(b) 200,000 to 450,000 per cu. mm
(c) 200,000 to 400,000 per cu. mm
(d) 250,000 to 450,000 per cu. mm
Answer. (b) 200,000 to 400,000 per cu. mm
Explanation:
Blood platelets are minute oval or round structure, non-nucleated, floating in blood. These are about 200,000 to 400,000 per cu. mm. of blood in an adult.

(viii) Bowman's capsule and Glomerulus are together known as Secondary capsule
(a) Proximal capsule
(b) None of these
(c) Malpighian capsule
Answer. (c) Malpighian capsule
Explanation:
Bowman's capsule and Glomerulus together called as Malpighian capsule or just renal capsule.

(ix) Regulation of blood supply in muscle is function of which hormone:
(a) Oxytocin
(b) Thyroxine
(c) Adrenaline
(d) Insulin
Answer. (c) Adrenaline
Explanation:
Adrenaline increases the blood supply to the muscle while decreasing it to skin and visceral organ.

(x) White matter mainly composed of:
(a) Myelinated Dendrites
(b) Myelinated Axons
(c) Myelinated Nerve cell bodies
(d) Unmyelinated Axons
Answer. (b) Myelinated Axon
Explanation:
White matter is the tissue present at the centre of the brain. It is light in colour because of lipid(itchy substance) present in the myelin. It majorly composed of myelinated Axon. It is important because it allows messages to pass quickly between different area of gray matter. White matter continues to develop and peak in middle age.

(xi) Which of the following is the characteristic of artery?
(a) Blood flow uniformly
(b) Thin muscular wall

(c) Carry blood from organ to heart

(d) A narrow lumen

Answer. (d) A narrow lumen

Explanation:

An artery is a vessel which carries blood away from the heart towards any organ. It has thick muscular wall a narrow lumen (the central bore), and the blood in it flows in spurts which correspond to the ventricular contractions of the heart.

(xii) Sheet of fiber that connects two cerebral hemisphere called:

(a) Thalamus

(b) Corpus callosum

(c) Medulla oblongata

(d) Pons

Answer. (b) Corpus callosum

Explanation:

Corpus callosum (hard body) is a sheet of fibers connecting the two cerebral hemispheres. Its function is to transfer information from one hemisphere to other.

(xiii) Sensory neuron is not needed in

(a) Involuntary action

(b) Voluntary action

(c) Controlled reflex action

(d) Uncontrolled reflex action

Answer. (a) Involuntary action

Explanation:

Sensory nerve is only needed when there is voluntary action is going on not when there is involuntary action. Sensory nerve is present around sensory organs.

(xiv) Body temperature is regulated by:

(a) Thalamus

(b) Cerebellum

(c) Hypothalamus

(d) Medulla

Answer. (c) Hypothalamus

Explanation:

Hypothalamus is part of brain (Fore brain). It controls the hormonal secretions from endocrine glands. Hormone secreted from posterior pituitary gland secrete through it. This is the centre of hunger, thirst, body temperature control, love, hate etc. Blood pressure, metabolism of water, sweat, anger, joy etc. Are controlled by it.

(xv) Information is first acquired at

(a) Nerve Ending

(b) Dendrite
(c) Cell body
(d) Axon
Answer. (b) Dendrite
Explanation:
Information acquired at the end of the dendritic tip of the nerve cell sets off a chemical reaction that creates an electrical impulse.

Question 2

(i) Name the following: **[5]**

(a) The mineral element essential for the clotting of blood.
(b) The cells of the testes that produce male hormones.
(c) The nutritive layer of the eye which also prevents reflection of light.
(d) The structural and functional unit of the kidney.
(e) That part of the chloroplast where the light reaction of photosynthesis takes place.

Answer.
(a) Calcium
(b) Leydig/interstitial cells
(c) Choroid
(d) Nephron
(e) Grana

(ii) Given below is a set of five terms arrange and rewrite each set of terms in the correct order so as to be in logical sequence **[5]**

(a) Water molecules, oxygen, grana, hydrogen, hydroxyl ions and protons
(b) Right auricle, left ventricle, vena cava, pulmonary vein, lungs, right ventricle, pulmonary artery, aorta, left. Auricle
(c) Graafian follicle , oviducal funnel, fallopian tube, ovum uterus
(d) Metaphase, telophase, prophase, anaphase, interphase
(e) Spongy cell, upper epidermis, stoma, palisade tissues, sub stomatal space.

Answer.
(a) According to the logical sequence of the photosynthesis :-
(Protons, grana, water molecules, hydrogen ions, oxygen).
(b) Right auricle, left ventricle, vena cava, pulmonary vein, lungs, right ventricle, pulmonary artery, aorta, left Auricle:-
(Vena cava, right auricle, right ventricle, pulmonary veins, left auricle, left ventricles, aorta).
(c) Graafian follicle , oviducal funnel, fallopian tube, ovum uterus:-
(Ovum uterus, Graafian follicle. Oviducal funnel, fallopian tube, uterus).
(d) Metaphase, telophase, prophase, anaphase, interphase:-
(Interphase, metaphase, prophase, anaphase, telophase).
(e) Spongy cell, upper epidermis, stoma, palisade tissues, sub stomatal space:-

(Upper epidermis, palisade, spongy ell, sub stomatal space, stomata)

(iii) Match the items given in Column I with the most appropriate ones in Column II and rewrite the correct matching pairs. **[5]**

Column A	Column B
(a) Pituitary gland	i. Testosterone
(b) Sulphur dioxide	ii. Calcium
(c) Seminiferous tubules	iii. Growth hormone
(d) Clotting of blood	iv. Acid rain
(e) Guttation	v. Sperms
	vi. Global warming
	vii. Magnesium
	viii. Hydathodes

Answer.

Column A	Column B
(a) Pituitary gland	Growth hormone
(b) Sulphur dioxide	Acid rain
(c) Seminiferous tubules	Sperms
(d) Clotting of blood	Calcium
(e) Guttation	Hydathodes

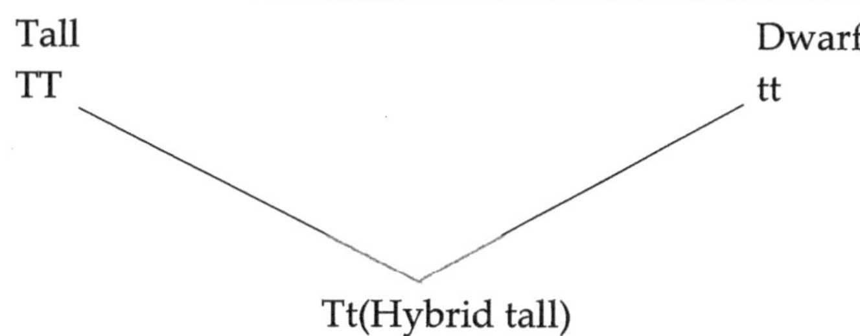

(iv) Choose the odd one out from the following terms and name the category to which the others belong: **[5]**

(a) Haemoglobin, Glucagon, Iodopsin, Rhodopsin.

(b) Urethra, Uterus, Urinary Bladder, Ureter.

(c) Transpiration, Photosynthesis, Phagocytosis, Guttation.

(d) Cyton, Photon, Axon, Dendron.

(e) Oxytocin, Insulin, Prolactin, Progesterone.

Answer.

(a) Odd term: Glucagon
Category: Body pigments

(b) Odd term: Uterus
Category: Urinary system

(c) Odd term: Phagocytosis

Category: Process in plants

(d) Odd term: Photon

Category: Parts of a neuron

(e) Odd term: Insulin

Category: Female hormones

(v) Mention the exact location of the following structures:

(a) Thylakoids

(b) Organ of Corti

(c) Lenticels

(d) Bicuspid valve

(e) Loop of Henle.

Answer:

(a) In the stroma of chloroplasts.

(b) In the interior of cochlea.

(c) Small apertures on the surface of corky stem.

(d) Guarding the opening between the left auricle and left ventricle of the heart.

(e) Between proximal and distal convoluted tubules of the nephrons (uriniferous tubules) of the kidney.

Section B

(Attempt any four questions)

Question 3

(i) Define Monohybrid cross **[1]**

Answer. A Monohybrid cross is one in which two pure breeding individuals involving one pair of contrasting traits are crossed or bred. For example, the cross between a homozygous dominant parent (TT) and a homozygous recessive parent (tt) would produce the F1 generation of a hybrid progeny expressing the dominant trait (Tt).

(ii) Give one difference between Guttation and Bleeding. **[2]**

Answer.

Guttation	Bleeding
It occurs due to escape of water in form of water droplets through hydathodes.	It occurs due flow of plant sap from the site of injury or cut.

(iii) What is blood vessel? Give two examples. **[2]**

Answer

Blood vessels are the branched tubes that extend from the heart to all parts of the body. Three main types of blood vessels carry blood towards and away from the heart. These are arteries, veins and capillaries.

(a) Artery is a blood vessel whose function is to carry blood away from the heart towards any other organ. An artery is comprised of thick walls and a narrow central lumen.

(b) Vein is a type of blood vessel that carries blood away from the organs towards the heart. It is comprised of thinner walls and a large central lumen.

(c) Capillary is a narrow tube-like blood vessel, comprised of single layer of endothelial cells. Capillaries can contract and dilate with the decrease and increase in the blood supply to various body parts.

(iv) State the main function of the lymphocytes of blood. **[2]**

Answer. The main function of the lymphocytes of blood is to produce antibodies

.

(v) The diagram given below is that of a structure present in a human kidney. **[3]**

Study the same and answer the questions that follows:

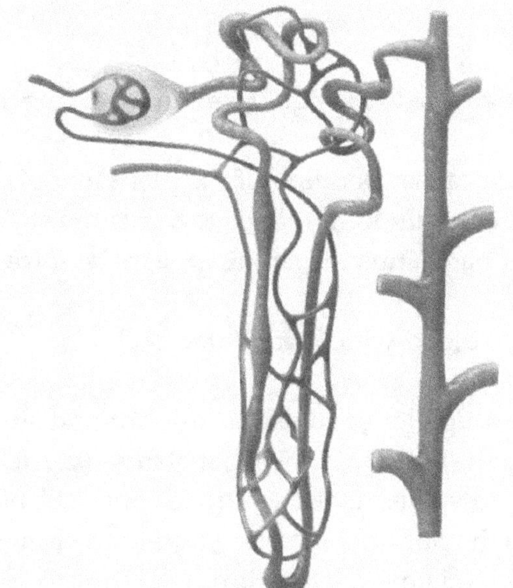

(a) Name the structure represented in the digram.

(b) What is the liquid entering part ' 1 ' called?

Name two substances present in this liquid that are re-absorbed in the tubule.

(c) What is the fluid that comes to part ' 2 ' called?

Name the main nitrogenous waste in it.

(d) Mention the three main steps involved in the formation of the fluid mentioned in (iii) above.

(e) Name the substance which may be present in the fluid part ' 2 ' if a person suffers from diabetes mellitus.

Answer.

(a) Renal tubule or Nephron

(b) Glomerular filtrate

Water, glucose

(c) Urine

Urea

(d) Ultrafiltration, Selective reabsorption, Tubular secretion

(e) Glucose

Question 4

(i) Expand the abbreviation of ADP **[1]**

Answer. Adenosine diphosphate

(ii) Name the three eye defects. **[2]**

Answer.

There are three common eye defects, and they are

(i) Myopia or near-sightedness,

(ii) Hypermetropia or far-sightedness, and

(iii) Presbyopia.

(iii) Shoot of the plant bends towards the light.Explain by giving suitable reasons. **[2]**

Answer.

Auxin is the hormone that causes bending of the plant towards light. Auxin synthesized by the cells present in area receiving light moves towards the shady side of the stem and causes elongation of that part. Thus the shoot appears bent towards light.

(iv) Mention two pathways of blood which circulated by heart. **[2]**

Answer.

Blood enters the heart through large veins, the inferior and superior vena cava, emptying oxygen-poor blood from the body into the right atrium (auricle) of the heart. Blood enters right ventricle via bicuspid valve. As the ventricle contracts, blood leaves the heart through the pulmonic valve, into the pulmonary artery and to the lungs where it is oxygenated. After getting oxygenated, blood enters left atrium (auricle) through pulmonary vein.

So, the correct option is 'Right auricle → Right ventricle → Lungs → left auricle → Left ventricle'.

(v) Study the following diagram carefully and then answer the questions that follow. The diagram is depicting a defect of the human eye: **[3]**

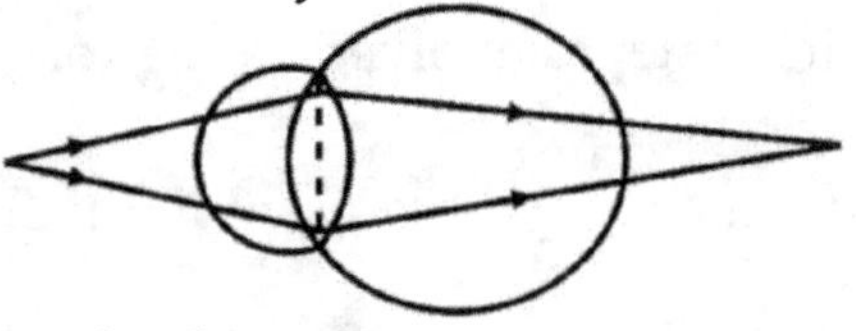

(i) Identify the defect shown in the diagram.

(ii) Give two possible reasons for the above defect.

(iii) Draw a neat labelled diagram to show how the above defect can be rectified. (5)

Answer. (i) Long sightedness or hypermetropia.

(ii) **(a)** The lens is flattened.

(b) The eyeball is shortened from front to back.

(iii) Hypermetropia corrected

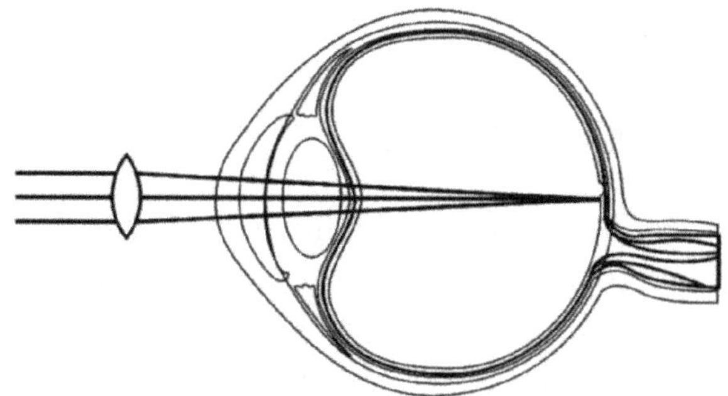

Question 5

(i) Define-Pulmonary semilunar valve **[1]**

Answer. Semilunar valves are present between the ventricles and major heart arteries. It allows the flow of blood from the right atrium to the right ventricle and the left atrium to the left ventricle. It allows the flow of blood from the left ventricle to the aorta and the right ventricle to the pulmonary artery.

(ii) Explain the importance of carbon dioxide for **[2]**

(a) Photosynthesis

(b) warming the earth's environment. State what would happen if excess carbon dioxide as a pollutant is released into the atmosphere.

Answer. (a) In photosynthesis, green plants manufacture their own food by absorbing carbon dioxide in the air and make food in the presence of chlorophyll and sunlight.

$$\underset{\text{(in air)}}{\text{Carbon dioxide}} + \text{Water} \xrightarrow[\text{chlorophyll}]{\text{sunlight}} \underset{\text{(glucose)}}{\text{carbohydrates}} + \text{oxygen}$$

In the greenhouse effect, earth gets heated up because of infrared, visible ray & ultra violet rays. Carbon dioxide in the air allows UV rays to pass through but prevents the infrared rays from being radiated out of earth's surface. It results in warming the earth's environment.

(b) If excess carbon dioxide is released into the atmosphere, it will result in rise in temperature leading to global warming.

(iii) What is the significance of Calvin cycle in plant? **[2]**

Answer. The main purpose of the Calvin Cycle is to produce three carbon sugars that can be used to make other sugar molecules such as starch, glucose, and cellulose. These sugars are used by plants for making other structures. In the calvin cycle, carbon is directly taken from the air and is converted to the plant matter.

(iv) What is abscissic acid? Explain it's role in plant. **[2]**

Answer. It is a growth-inhibiting hormone. Abscisic acid causes dormancy in seeds and buds that's why it was formerly known as dormin. It promotes ageing or senescence of leaves and in shedding of leaves. Conditions like high temperature, salinity, drought etc.

(v) Give the schematic representation of cell cycle. **[3]**

Answer. Cell cycle:

The cll cycle is a cycle of stages that cells pass through to allow them to divide and produce new cells.

The graphic shows a visual representation of the cell cycle. The small section labelled "M" represents mitosis, while interphase is shown subdivided into its major components: the G1, S, and G2 phases.

G1 phase. Metabolic changes prepare the cell for division. At a certain point - the restriction point - the cell is committed to division and moves into the S phase.

S phase. DNA synthesis replicates the genetic material. Each chromosome now consists of two sister chromatids.

G2 phase. Metabolic changes assemble the cytoplasmic materials necessary for mitosis and cytokinesis.

M phase. A nuclear division (mitosis) followed by a cell division (cytokinesis).

The period between mitotic divisions - that is, G1, S and G2 - is known as interphase.

Question 6

(i) Define-systolic pressure **[1]**

Answer. When heart pumps, the blood pressure exerted against by the artery walls is called as systolic blood pressure. The pressure exerted by blood against by the vessels when heart is at resting stage between beats is called as diastolic blood pressure.

(ii) Differentiate between Rod and Cones with reference to colour differentiation. **[2]**

Comparison of rods & cones

Rods	Cones
Used for seotopic vision (vision under low light conditions)	Used for photopic vision (vision under high light conditions)
Very light sensitive; sensitive to scattered light	Not very light sensitive; sensitive to only direct light
Loss causes night blindness	Loss causes legal blindness
Low visual acuity	High visual acuity; better spatial resolution
Not present in fovea	Concentrated in fovea
2o times more rods than cones in the retina	
One type of photosensitive pigment	Three types of photosensitive pigment in humans
Confer achromatic vision	Confer color vision

(iii) State the function of plant hormones with a suitable example. **[2]**

Answer: The four types of plant hormones are:

(a) Auxins - It promotes cell enlargement and cell differentiation in plants.
(b) Gibberellins - It helps in breaking the dormancy in seeds and buds.
(c) Cytokinin's - It promotes cell division in plants.
(d) Abscisic acid - It promotes the dormancy in seeds and buds.

(iv) X-Linked disorders is generally seen in males. Explain **[2]**

Answer: This is because: Males have only 1X chromosome, from their mother. If that X chromosome has the gene for redgreen color blindness (instead of a normal X chromosome), they will have red-green color blindness. Females have 2X chromosomes, one from their mother and one from their father.

Question 7

(i) The diagram shows the Excretory System of a Human being. Study the same and then answer the questions that follow: **[2]**

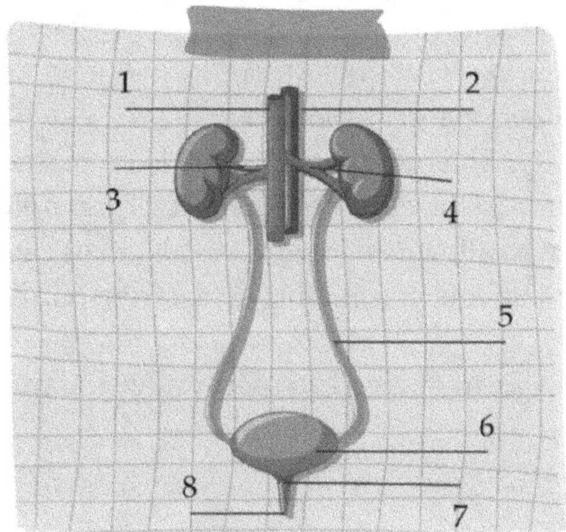

(a) Name the parts labelled 1, 2, 3 and 4 .
(b) Give the main function of the parts labelled 5,6,7 and 8 .
(c) Name the endocrine gland which could be added in the diagram and state its location/position.

Answer. (a) 1-Vena cava, 2-Dorsal aorta, 3-Renal artery, 4-Renal vein.

(b) 5-Ureter are tubes which connect kidneys with urinary bladder. 6-Urinary bladder stores urine temporarily. 7-Spincter muscles control the opening and closing of urinary bladder.8-Urethra is the connection between urinary bladder and external opening of urinary tract.

(c) Adrenal glands are present at the anterior end of the kidneys.

Question 8

(i) Explain – Photosynthesis **[1]**

Answer: Photosynthesis is a process by which phototrophs convert light energy into chemical energy, which is later used to fuel cellular activities. The chemical energy is stored in the form of sugars, which are created from water and carbon dioxide.

(ii) Give reasons how the rate of transpiration is affected by humidity of atmosphere. **[2]**

Answer: The humidity of the atmosphere:-

Transpiration is reduced if the air outside is humid. High humidity in the air reduces the rate of outward diffusion of the internal water vapour across stomata, thereby reducing the rate of transpiration.

(iii) Differentiate between cerebrum and spinal cord with respect to the arrangement of cytons and axons of neurons. **[2]**

Answer: Cerebrum: The inner portion of the cerebrum consists of white matter mainly containing the axons nerve fibres of the neurons. Spinal cord: The inner portion of the spinal cord consists of gray matter containing the cell bodies motor and associated neurons whereas the white matter forms outer layer.

(iv) State how sunlight affects transpiration. **[2]**

Answer: Light intensity: The transpiration rate is increased due to the increase in light intensity. During daytime in the sunlight, the rate of transpiration is faster. This is because the stomata remains open to allow the inward diffusion of carbon dioxide for photosynthesis. During dark, the stomata are closed, and hence transpiration hardly occurs at night.

(v) Given below is the diagram of a cell as seen under the microscope after having bess. placed in a solution: **[3]**

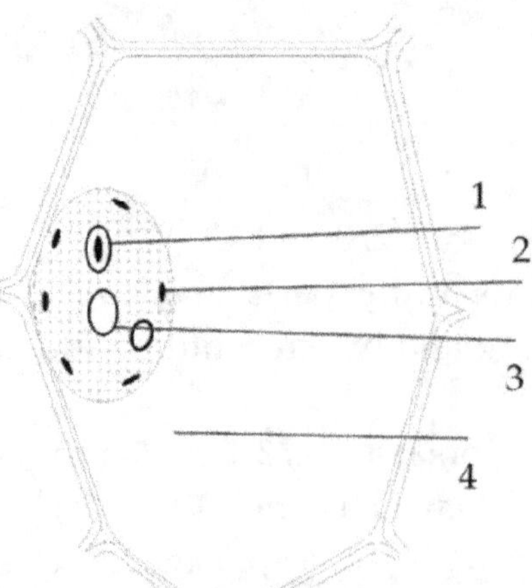

(a) What is the technical term used for the state/condition of the cell given abould

(b) Give the technical term for the solution in which the cell was placed.

(c) Name the parts numbered 1 to 4.

(d) Is the cell given above a plant cell or an animal cell? Give two reasons in support of your answer as evident from the diagram.

(e) What would you do to bring this cell back to its original condition?

Answer. (i) Plasmolysis.

(ii) Hypertonic solution.

(iii) 1-Nucleus
2 - Cell organelle
3-Vacuole
4-Strong hypertonic solution

(iv) It is a plant cell because firstly plant cells are angular in shape and animal cells are spherical in shape. Secondly, plant cells have a cell wall which is clearly shown in the above diagram, animal cells don't have a cell wall.

(v) If cell is kept in water for some time it can be brought back to its original condition.

Question 9

(i) Define-XX and XY **[1]**

Answer: These are sex chromosomes. females have an XX pair of chromosomes, male have an XY pair of chromosomes . A baby's gender is determined by these chromosomes.

(ii) Grapes shrink when immersed in a very strong sugar solution." Explain **[2]**

Answer: Very strong sugar solution is hypertonic to the grapes juice. Therefore, water from inside the grapes moves to outside hypertonic solution. It results shrinkage of the grapes.

(iii) What is the difference between temporary and permanent wilting? **[2]**

Temporary Wilting	Permanent Wilting
Temporary drooping of young leaves and shoots due to loss of turgidity especially during noon.	State of permanent loss of turgidity in leaves and other parts of plant.
Occurs when rate of transpiration is more than water absorption due to shrinkage of roots.	Rate of transpiration is more than rate of absorption, but difference is below critical level.
Wilting recovers as soon as water is re-plenished in the soil around root hairs.	Wilting is not recovered as cells do not re-gain their turgidity even in presence of plentiful water and atmosphere.
Plant regains its normal growth.	Plant eventually dies.

(iv) Explain two reasons for the high birth rate in India. **[2]**

Answer: The birth rate measures the number of birth during a year per 1000 of population. India experiences a higher birth rate comparatively. Birth rate in India is high because of the following reasons- illiteracy, social orthodoxy, and desire of a male child.

(v) The diagrams given below show the cross section of two kinds of blood vessels:

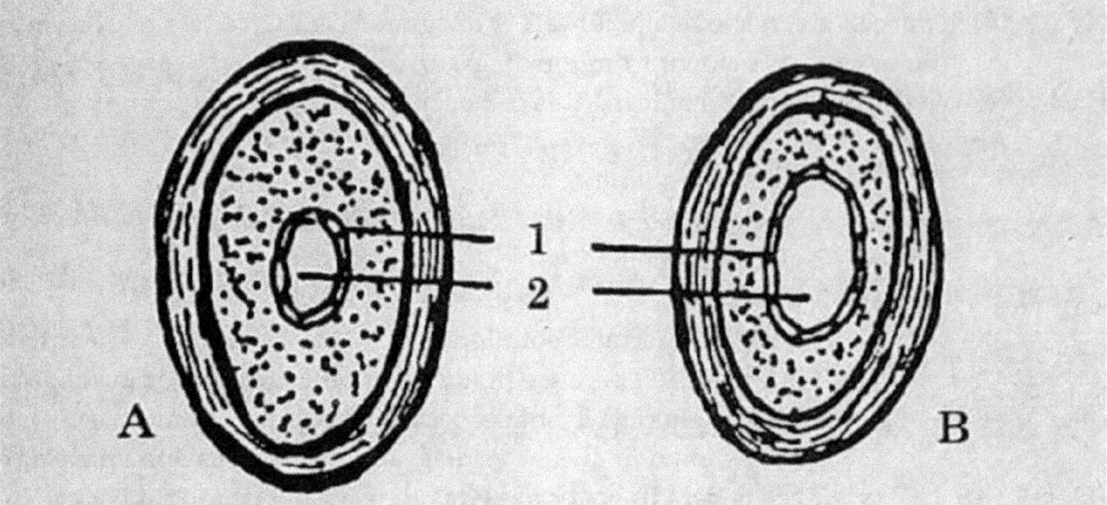

(a) Identify the blood vessels *A* and *B*. In each case give a reason to support your answer.

(b) Name the parts numbered 1 and 2.

(c) When are the sounds "LUBB" and "DUP" produced during a heartbeat?

(d) Name the blood vessel that

i. begins and ends in capillaries.

ii. supplies blood to the walls of the heart.

Answer (a) A-Artery, B-Vein. Reason for indentification:

Artery has thick wall and narrow lumen while vein has thin wall and broad lumen.

(b) 1-Endothelium, 2-Lumen.

(c) "Lubb" is associated with ventricular systole while "Dup" is associated with ventricular diastole.

(d) i Portal vein.

ii Coronary artery.

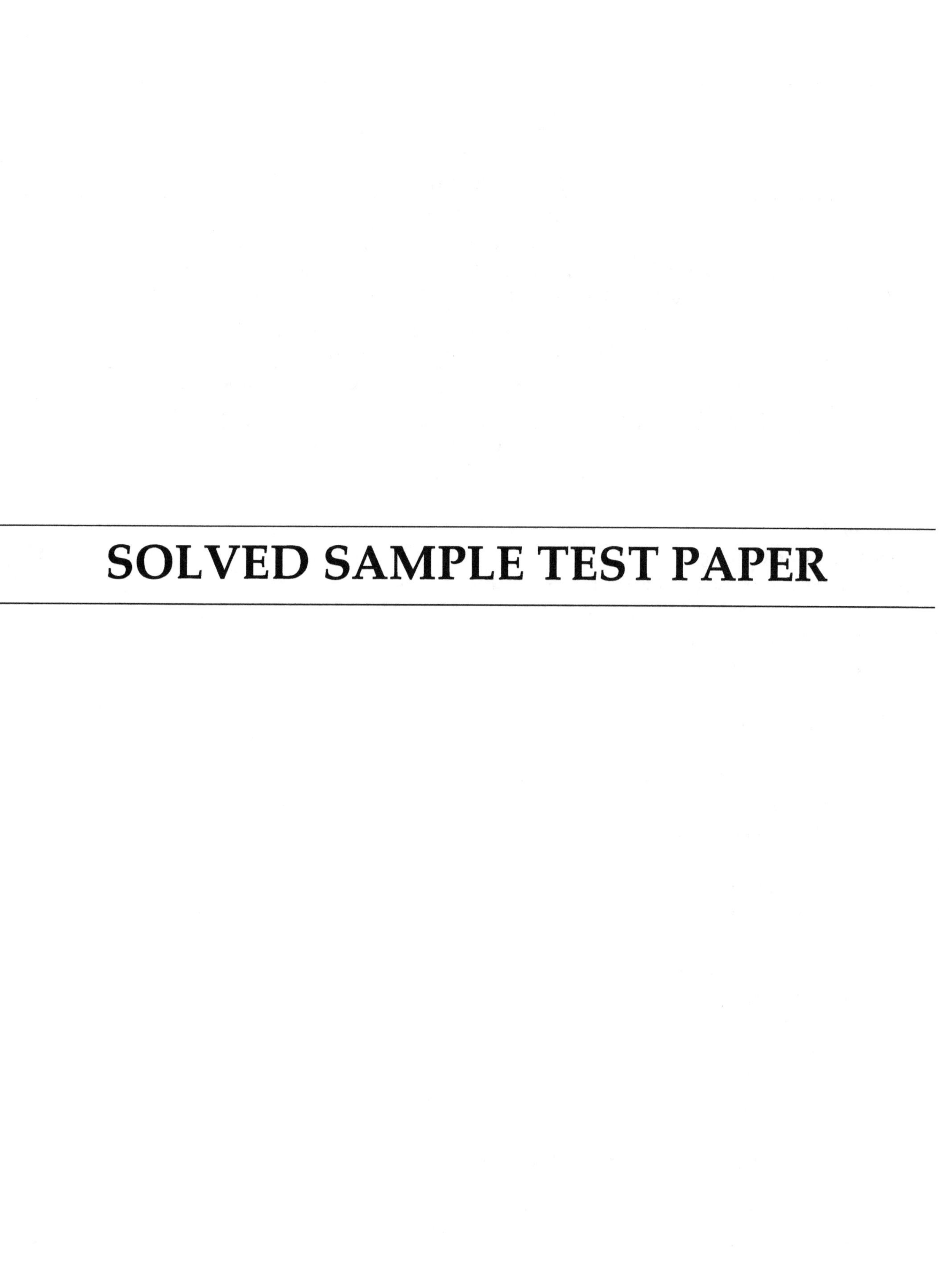

SOLVED SAMPLE TEST PAPER

ICSE 2023 EXAMINATION

SAMPLE TEST PAPER-1

BIOLOGY

(SCIENCE PAPER-2)

Maximum Marks: 80

Time allowed: Two hours

Answers to this Paper must be written on the paper provided separately.

You will not be allowed to write during first 15 minutes.

This time is to be spent in reading the question paper.

The time given at the head of this Paper is the time allowed for writing the answers.

(Section A is compulsory. Attempt any four questions from Section B.

The intended marks for questions or parts of questions are given in brackets [ ].

Section A

Answer all the questions from this section

Question 1

Choose the Correct Option **[15]**

(i) The process of meiosis takes place to produce

(a) Cells of the body.

(b) Cells of the brain.

(c) Sperms and ova.

(d) Testis and ovary

Ans: (c) Sperms and ova.

(ii) The alternate forms of the same genes are

(a) Alleles.

(b) Homozygous.

(c) A and b.

(d) none of these.

Ans. (a) Alleles.

(iii) Osmosis involves the movement of

(a) Turgidity

(b) Flaccidity

(c) Acidity

(d) None of these.

Ans. (a) Turgidity

(iv) The fluid-filled area of the chloroplast is the

(a) Grana.

(b) Stroma.

(c) Thylakoids.

(d) Membrane.
Ans. (b) Stroma

(v) Which hormone is secreted by the kidneys?
(a) Glucagon
(b) Insulin
(c) Rennin
(d) Renin
Ans. (d) Renin

(vi) The inability to see in the diffused light is due to
(a) Glaucoma.
(b) Cones.
(c) Rhodopsin.
(d) None of these.
Ans. (c) Rhodopsin.

(vii) The cerebral hemispheres in mammals are connected by
(a) Corpus luteum.
(b) Hypothalamus.
(c) Pons Varolii.
(d) Corpus callosum.
Ans. (a) Corpus luteum.

(viii) One of the effects of increased secretion of adrenaline is
(a) Dry mouth.
(b) Slowing of a heartbeat.
(c) Increases blood supply to muscles.
(d) None of these.
Ans. (a) Dry mouth.

(ix) Delta cells of the pancreas secrete
(a) Glucagon.
(b) Insulin.
(c) Somatostatin.
(d) Aldosteron
Ans. (c) Somatostatin.

(x) The life of the corpus luteum in case of no pregnancy is
(a) 4 days
(b) 10 days
(c) 14 days.

(d) 28 days
Ans. (b) 10 days

(xi) The cessation of menstruation in the female is termed
(a) Ovulation
(b) Menarche
(c) Menopause
(d) Parthenogenesis
Ans. (c) Menopause

(xii) The death rate of the population of a country is called
(a) Birth rate
(b) Mortality
(c) Sterility
(d) Natality
Ans. (b) Mortality

(xiii) Following industries emit heavy metals into the atmosphere:
(a) Steel manufacturing industries.
(b) Cement industries
(c) Petroleum refineries
(d) Paint and dye industries.
Ans. (c) Petroleum refineries

(xiv) The formation of urine in our excretory system is known as
(a) Haemopoiesis
(b) Uropoiesis
(c) Leucopoiesis
(d) None of these
Ans. (b) Uropoiesis

(xv) The Mitral valve is located
(a) Between right auricle and right ventricle
(b) At the origin of an aorta from the left ventricle
(c) Between the left auricle and left ventricle
(d) Between left and right auricles
Ans. (c) Between the left auricle and left ventricle

Question 2

(i) Name the following **[5]**
(a) Name the mitotic stage where chromosomes appear thread-like
(b) The two fluids that circulate in the body

(c) Iron contains respiratory pigment in erythrocytes
(d) An organic waste produced in man
(e) Defect arising due to shortening of the eyeball

(ii) Arrange and rewrite the terms in each group in the correct order so as to be in a logical sequence beginning with the term that is underlined. **[5]**

(a) Fibrin, Platelets, Thromboplastin, Fibrinogen, Thrombin
(b) Renal vein, renal artery, afferent arteriole, efferent arteriole, glomerulus.
(c) Receptor, Spinal cord, Effector, Motor neuron, Sensory neuron.
(d) Islets of Langerhans, pancreas, glucagon, α-cells, glycogenolysis
(e) Glomerulus, DCT, Henle's loop, PCT, Collecting duct.

(iii) Match the items given in Column I with the most appropriate ones in Column II and rewrite the correct matching pairs. **[5]**

Column-I	Column-II
Haemophilia	Gene
Johannsen	Sex-linked disease
Guttation	Potometer
Transpiration	Hydathodes
RBC	Leucocyte
	Thrombocyte
	Chromosome
	Erythrocyte

(iv) Choose the odd one out from the following terms and name the category to whiceh the others belong: **[5]**

(a) Cortisone, somatotropin, vasopressin. hormone,
(b) Dendrites, medullary sheath, axon, spinal cord.
(c) Renal artery, urinary bladder, kidney, ureter, urethra.
(d) Cytokinin, Auxin, Cytokine, Ethylene
(e) DNA, Chromosome, choroid, chromatid

(v) State the exact location of the following structures: **[5]**

(a) Iris
(b) Arachnoid
(c) Aortic semilunar valve
(d) Chlorophyll molecule

(e) Nephron

Section B

(Attempt any four questions from this Section.)

Question 3

(i) Define Micturition. [1]

(ii) Give one difference between cuticular and lenticular transpiration [2]

(iii) Natural and man-made pollution? Give one example. [2]

(iv) Give the significance of mitosis in an organism. [2]

(v) Given below is an experimental setup to study a particular process: [3]

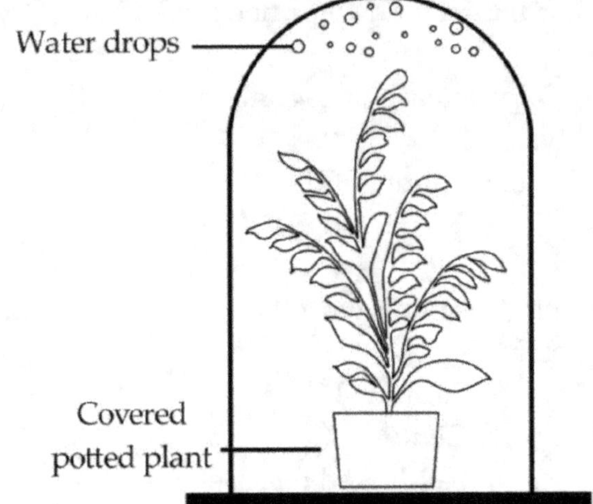

(a) Name the process being studied.

(b) Explain the process named in (a) above.

(c) Why is the pot covered with a plastic sheet?

(d) Mention one way in which this process is beneficial to the plant

(e) Suggest a suitable control for this experiment

Question 4

(i) Expand the abbreviation DNA [1]

(ii) Name two Y-linked disorders [2]

(iii) oil layered over water in the beaker. Explain by giving suitable reasons. [2]

(iv) What is the shape of the lens during near vision and distant vision? Explain. [2]

(v) Given below is a schematic diagram of a portion of DNA. [3]

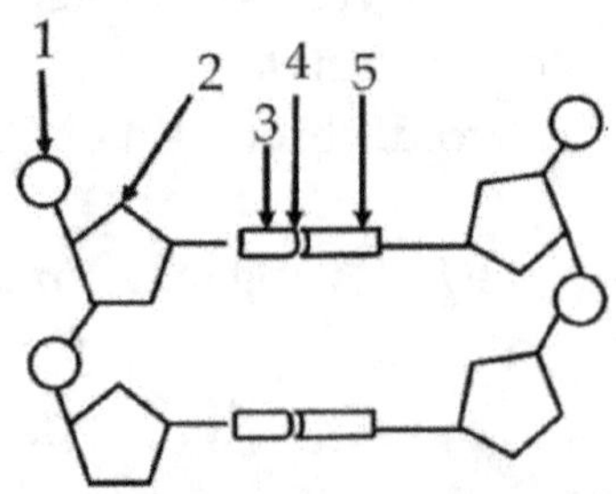

(a) How many strands it is showing?

(b) How many nucleotides have been shown in each strand?

(c) Name the parts numbered 1, 2, 3,4 and 5 respectively

(d) Name the DNA unit constituted by the parts 1,2 and 3 collectively.

Question 5

(i) Define- Osmoregulation. **[1]**

(ii) What is the significance of Mitosis? **[2]**

(iii) State two functions of the cornea. **[2]**

(iv) What is the importance of root hair in plants? **[2]**

(v) Draw a neat labeled diagram of the eye and the formation of an image of an object inside the eye. **[3]**

Question 6

(i) Define-Allele **[1]**

(ii) Differentiate between Pulmonary circulation and Systemic circulation with reference to blood circulation. **[2]**

(iii) State the function of ciliary muscles with suitable examples **[2]**

(iv) Hypertrichosis is generally seen in males. Explain. **[2]**

(v) The diagram below represents the structure found in the inner ear. Study the same and then answer the questions that follow:- **[3]**

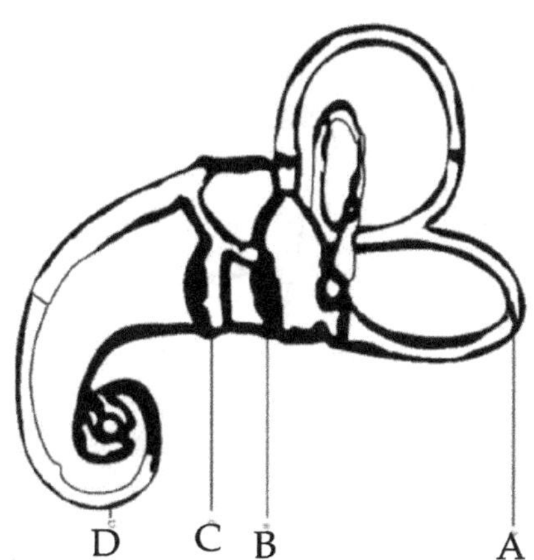

(a) Name the parts labelled A, B, C and D.

(b) Name the part of the ear responsible for transmitting impulses to the brain.

(c) Name the part labelled above which is responsible for:

i Static equilibrium:

ii Dynamic equilibrium.

iii Hearing.

(d) Name the audio receptor cells which pick up vibrations.

(e) Name the fluid nresent in the inner ear

Question 7

(i) Define – Photolysis [1]

(ii) Write a small paragraph on the uses of artificial kidneys. [2]

(iii) Mention any two points in which photosynthesis and respiration in plants differ from each other. [2]

(iv) What is the difference between systole and diastole [2]

(v) Draw a neat labeled diagram of the human heart in a median vertical section. [3]

Question 8

(i) Define - Pacemaker

(ii) The release of urine is called micturition, the neural mechanism causing it. How the micturition takes place. Explain.

(iii) Differentiate between hyperglycemia and hypoglycemia.

(iv) State two harmful effects of ozone depletion.

(v) Study the same and then answer the questions that follow:

(a) Name the factor being studied in this experiment?

(b) Why was the plant kept in a dark room before conducting the experiment?

(c) Why was the experimental leaf then kept in

i boiling water

ii methylated spirit?

(d) Name the solution used to test for presence of starch in the leaf.

(e) What will we observe in the experimental leaf at the end of the starch test?

(f) Give a balanced chemical equation to represent the process of photosynthesis.

ICSE 2023 EXAMINATION

SAMPLE TEST PAPER-2

BIOLOGY

(SCIENCE PAPER-2)

Maximum Marks: 80

Time allowed: Two hours

Answers to this Paper must be written on the paper provided separately.

You will not be allowed to write during first 15 minutes.

This time is to be spent in reading the question paper.

The time given at the head of this Paper is the time allowed for writing the answers.

(Section A is compulsory. Attempt any four questions from Section B.

The intended marks for questions or parts of questions are given in brackets [ ].

Section A

Answer all the questions from this section

Question 1. **[15]**

(i) A cell has 7 pairs of chromosomes. After mitotic division, the number of chromosome pairs in the daughter cells would be

(a) 3/12

(b) 14

(c) 70

(d) 7

Answer (d) 7

(ii) The characters in an individual always appear, whenever present are called

(a) Recessive characters

(b) Dominant characters

(c) Genotypic characters

(d) Phenotypic characters

Answer (b) Dominant characters

(iii) Osmosis involves the movement of

(a) Suspended particles from lower to higher concentrations

(b) Suspended particles from higher to lower concentration

(c) Water from the more concentrated solution to the less concentrated solution

(d) Water from the less concentrated solution to the more concentrated solution

Answer (c) Water from the more concentrated solution to the less concentrated solution

(iv) In which of the following plants there will be no transpiration?

(a) Aquatic, submerged plants

(b) Plants are found in deserts

(c) Aquatic plants with floating leaves

(d) Plants growing in hilly regions

Answer (a) Aquatic, submerged plants

(v) If the rate of transpiration becomes more than the rate of photosynthesis plants will
(a) Continue to live, but will not be able to store food
(b) Be killed instantly
(c) Grow more vigorously because more energy will be available
(d) Stop growing and gradually die of starvation
Answer (d) Stop growing and gradually die of starvation

(vi) The chloroplasts contain all these except
(a) Grana
(b) Cristae
(c) Stroma
(d) Thylakoids
Answer (b) Cristae

(vii) Which of the following cell leads to the formation of the endocrine part of the Pancreas?
(a) Islets of Langerhans
(b) Medulla
(c) Cartilage
(d) Interstitial cell
Answer (a) Islets of Langerhans

(viii) Towards which side of the figure is the heart located?
(a) Chest cavity
(b) Bottom side
(c) Left side
(d) Right side
Answer (a) Chest cavity

(ix) A muscular wall is absent in:
(a) Capillary
(b) Arteriole
(c) Venule
(d) Vein
Answer (a) Capillary

(x) The hepatic portal system starts from
(a) digestive system to the liver
(b) kidney to liver
(c) liver to heart
(d) liver to kidney

Answer (a) Digestive system to the liver

(xi) Non-desiring couples or in the event of some serious disease forced abortion is carried out by doctors. The procedure is known as

(a) Intrauterine device.

(b) Surgical method.

(c) Medical termination of pregnancy.

(d) None of the above

Answer (b) Surgical method.

(xii) The prime source of CFCs

(a) Vehicular emissions.

(b) Industrial effluents.

(c) Domestic sewage.

(d) Refrigeration equipment.

Answer (d) Refrigeration equipment.

(xiii) Which of the following parts of the human ear contribute to hearing?

(a) Cochlea, ear ossicles and tympanum

(b) Semicircular canals, utriculus and sacculus

(c) Eustachian tube, tympanum and utriculus

(d) Perilymph, ear ossicles and semicircular canals

Answer (a) Cochlea, ear ossicles and tympanum

(xiv) Hyposecretion of hormones from the adrenal cortex causes

(a) Cushing's syndrome

(b) Addison's disease

(c) Hypoglycemia

(d) Both (b) and (c)

Answer (a) Cushing's syndrome

(xv) The production of starch, and not glucose, is often used as a measure of photosynthesis in leaves because.

(a) Starch is the immediate product of photosynthesis.

(b) Glucose formed in photosynthesis soon gets converted into starch.

(c) Starch is soluble in water.

(d) Sugar cannot be tested.

Answer (b) Glucose formed in photosynthesis soon gets converted into starch.

Question 2.

(i) Name the following: **[5]**

(a) The chromosome number in the daughter cells.

(b) The three components of a nucleotide.

(c) The process by which molecules distribute themselves evenly within the space they occupy.

(d) The hormone increases blood pressure.

(e) The chemical element caused minamata disease in Japan.

Answer

(a) 46

(b) Sugar, Base and phosphate

(c) Diffusion

(d) Urotensin, endothelins, angiotensin

(e) Methylmercury(MeHg)

(ii) Arrange and rewrite the terms in each group in the correct order so as to be in a logical sequence beginning with the term that is underlined. **[5]**

(a) Puberty, menopause, menstrual, menarche, reproductive age.

(b) The cochlea, tympanum, auditory canal, ear ossicles, and oval window.

(c) Afferent arteriole, renal vein, capillary network, glomerulus, efferent arteriole.

(d) water molecules, oxygen, grana, hydrogen, and hydroxyl ions, photons.

(e) Sperm duct, penis, testes, sperms, semen.

Answer

(a) 2,5,4,3,1

(b) 5,2,1,3,4

(c) 1,4,5,2,3

(d) 3,2,4,5,1

(e) 3,1,2,4

(iii) Match the items given in Column I with the most appropriate ones in Column II and rewrite the correct matching pairs. **[5]**

Column I		Column II
(a) Cardiac cycle	i	Defective haemoglobin in RBC
(b) Sickle cell anemia	ii	0.85sec
(c) Allele	iii	Chromosome similar in size and shape
(d) Genetics	iv	Alternative forms of a gene
(e) Homologous chromosome	v	Study of laws of inheritance
	vi	Character and trait defective WBC

Answer

(a) ii

(b) i

(c) iv

(d) v

(e) iii

(iv) Choose the odd one out from the following terms and name the category to which the others belong: **[5]**

(a) CO_2, bile pigments, water, excretion, urea.

(b) Iodine, cretinism, goiter, myxoedema.

(c) Oestrogen; progestrone; testosterone; prolactin.

(d) Dendrites, medullary sheath, axon, spinal cord.

(e) Basophils, neutrophils, monocytes, eosinophils.

Answer

(a) Excretion

(b) Iodine

(c) Prolactin

(d) spinal cord

(e) monocytes

(v) State the exact location of the following structures: **[5]**

(a) Cilary body

(b) Umbilical cord

(c) Granum

(d) Centrosome

(e) Adrenal gland

Answer

(a) Behind the iris

(b) Attached to the foetus

(c) Inside the belly button

(d) Outside the nucleus but often near to it

(e) on top of both kidneys

Section B

(Attempt any four questions from this Section)

Question 3.

(i) Define Endosmosis **[1]**

(ii) Give differences between exocrine and endocrine glands. **[2]**

(iii) What is Tonicity? Explain with the help of examples. **[2]**

(iv) State Mendel's Law of Dominance **[2]**

(v) Given below is an apparatus used to study a particular process in plants. Study the same and answer the question that follow: **[3]**

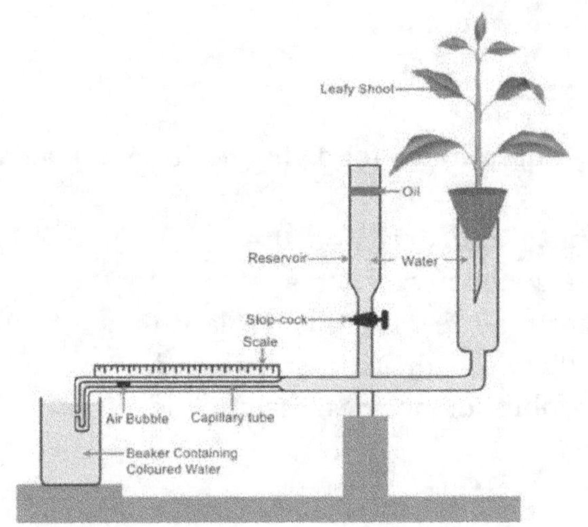

(a) Name the apparatus.

(b) Mention one limitation of this apparatus.

(c) What happens to the movement of the air bubble if the apparatus is kept:

i In the dark

ii In sunlight

iii In front of a fan?

Question 4.

(i) Define the Dominant trail. **[1]**

(ii) Name Two valves of the heart. **[2]**

(iii) Plants have no blood, yet we sometimes say that a plant is "bleeding". How do you justify this?

(iv) List any four advantages of transpiration to the plant. **[2]**

(v) A family consists of two parents and their five children and the pedigree chart below shows the inheritance of the trait colour-blindness. [3]

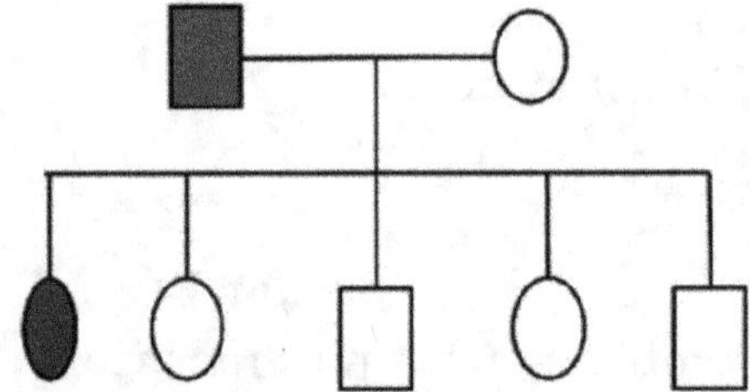

(a) Who is colour blind in the parents - Father or Mother?

(b) How many daughters and sons have been born in the family?

(c) What does the child 1 indicate about this trait?

(d) Complete the depiction of all probabilities if the trait among the children 25 in the chart.

(e) On which chromosome s the gene of this trait located?

(f) Name one other trait in humans which follows the similar pattern of inheritance

Question 5.

(i) Define Variations [1]

(ii) Differentiate between Turgidity and Flaccidity in terms of soil water. [2]

(iii) State the function of the spinal cord With suitable examples [2]

(iv) Is it correct to say that the testes produce testosterone? Discuss? [2]

(v) Draw a neat labeled diagram to show the vertical section of the human female reproductive system. [3]

Question 6.

(i) Define Puberty [1]

(ii) Differentiate between cowpeas gland and prostrate gland with reference to secretion. [2]

(iii) State the function of stomata with a suitable example. [2]

(iv) Blood vessels enter and leave the heart. Explain. [2]

(v) The diagram given below depicts the cross section of the spinal cord. Study the same and then answer the question that follow: [3]

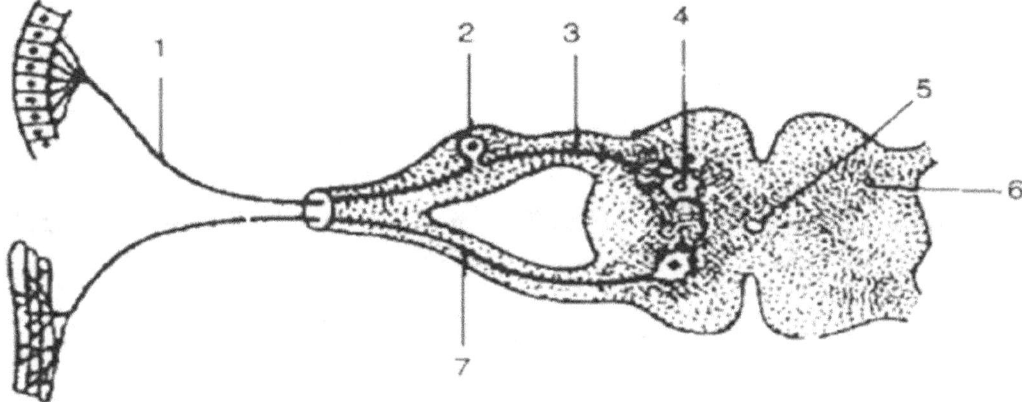

(a) Name the process that is being depicted.

(b) Name the parts labelled 2, 5 and 6 .

(c) Name the cells in contact with the part labelled 1.

(d) What is the function of the parts labelled 3, 4 and 7? What is the technical term given to the pathway represented by 3,4 and 7 ?

(e) How does the arrangement of cells in the spinal cord differ from that in the brain?

Question 7.

(i) Explain Myocardial infarction. [1]

(ii) How are carbon dioxide and urea, excreted by the fetus, removed? Explain. [2]

(iii) Mention two functions of dendrites. [2]

(iv) What is the difference between a yellow spot and a blind spot? [2]

(v) Draw a neat labeled diagram showing the pathway of water through leaf cells. [3]

Question 8.

(i) Define- sunken stomata [1]

(ii) Experiments to prove that carbon dioxide is necessary for photosynthesis explain [2]

(iii) Differentiate between Arteries and Veins.

(iv) State two important effects of plant hormone "Auxin" [2]

(v) The following diagram is a setup to demonstrate an experiment: [3]

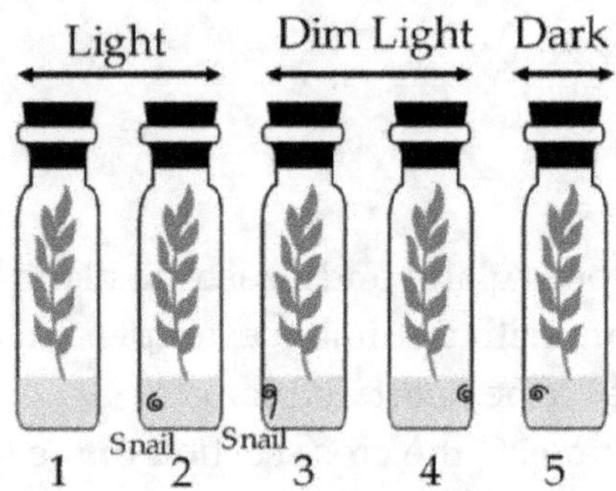

(a) In which tube would you expect the greatest increase in dry weight of the poudweed?

i 1
ii 2
iii 3
iv 4
v 5

(b) In which tube would you expect to find the plant with the least amount of starch?

i 1
ii 2
iii 3
iv 4
v 5

(c) The tube in which most oxygen would be found is:

i 1
ii 2
iii 3
iv 4
v 5

(d) The tube in which least carbon dioxide would be found is:

i 1
ii 2
iii 3
iv 4
v 5

(e) The tube in which the plant would survive for the shortest length of time is:

i 1
ii 2
iii 3
iv 4
v 5

(vi) Pondweed was placed in five water-filled tubes. The experiment was setup as shown in the diagram. The tubes were then left for 24 hours.

(vii) Write the correct answer out of the five available choices given under each question:

ICSE 2023 EXAMINATION

SAMPLE TEST PAPER-3

BIOLOGY

(SCIENCE PAPER-2)

Maximum Marks: 80

Time allowed: Two hours

Answers to this Paper must be written on the paper provided separately.

You will not be allowed to write during first 15 minutes.

This time is to be spent in reading the question paper.

The time given at the head of this Paper is the time allowed for writing the answers.

(Section A is compulsory. Attempt any four questions from Section B.

The intended marks for questions or parts of questions are given in brackets [ ].

Section A

Answer all the questions from this section

Question 1. **[15]**

(i) The division of the cytoplasm in cells is called

(a) Karyokinesis

(b) Cytokinesis

(c) Cell division.

(d) Meiosis.

Answer (b) Cytokinesis

(ii) The transmission of the characters from the parent to the offspring is called

(a) Variation.

(b) Genetics.

(c) Heredity.

(d) None of these.

Answer(c) Heredity

(iii) The process by which raisins swell up when placed in a beaker of water is called

(a) Osmosis.

(b) Active transport.

(c) Diffusion.

(d) Passive transport.

Answer(a) Osmosis.

(iv) The organic molecule produced directly by photosynthesis is

(a) Lipid,

(b) Sugar.

(c) Amino acid.

(d) DNA

Answer(b) Sugar.

(v) Which one of these reactions occurs during photosynthesis?

(a) Carbon dioxide is reduced and water is oxidized.

(b) Water is reduced and carbon dioxide is oxidized.

(c) Carbon dioxide and water are both oxidized.

(d) Carbon dioxide and water are both reduced.

Answer(a). Carbon dioxide is reduced and water is oxidized.

(vi) Role of auxin in plant

(a) Elongation of node

(b) Apical dominance

(c) Cell division

(d) Ripening

Answer(b). Apical dominance

(vii) Agranulocytes are:

(a) Lymphocytes, Monocytes

(b) Lymphocytes, Basophils

(c) Eosinophils, Basophils

(d) Eosinophils, Monocytes

Answer(a). Lymphocytes, Monocytes

(viii) The structural and functional unit of excretion in the human kidney is the:

(a) Ureter

(b) Bowman's capsule

(c) Renal pelvis

(d) Nephron

Answer(d). Nephron

(ix) The nephron discharges their urine at the

(a) Urinary bladder

(b) Urethra

(c) Renal pelvis

(d) Renal pyramid

Answer(c) Renal pelvis

(x) The ventral root ganglion of the spinal cord contains cell bodies of the

(a) Motor neuron

(b) Sensory neuron

(c) Intermediate neuron

(d) Association neuron

Answer(a) Motor neuron

(xi) Which one of the following is mainly associated with the maintenance of the posture?

(a) Thalamus

(b) Pons

(c) Cerebrum

(d) Cerebellum

Answer(c) Cerebrum

(xii) Endocrine glands are also known as:

(a) Duct glands

(b) Bloodstream glands

(c) Ductless glands

(d) Duct form glands

Answer(c) Ductless glands

(xiii) Why is the right kidney at a slightly lower level than the left?

(a) Right kidney is slightly smaller.

(b) Left kidney is slightly smaller.

(c) Liver takes the much space of the right side.

(d) Pancreas takes the much of space on the right side.

Answer(c) Liver takes the much space of the right side.

(xiv) Name the phase of the cardiac cycle in which the auricles contract.

(a) Ventricular diastole

(b) Artery

(c) Diastole of atria

(d) Auricular systole

Answer(d) Auricular systole

(xv) The part of the human eye where rod cells and cone cells are located is the

(a) Retina

(b) Choroid

(c) Cornea

(d) Sclera

Answer(a) Retina

Question 2.

(i) Name the following **[5]**

(a) Mitotic stage where chromosomes appear thread-like.

(b) Name the pair of genes responsible for a particular characteristic in an individual.

(c) Phenomenon by which living or dead plant cells absorb water by surface attraction.

(d) Brain is formed by two types of substances

(e) Group of hormones which influence other endocrine glands to produce hormones.

(ii) Arrange and rewrite the terms in each group in the correct order to be in a logical sequence beginning with the term that is underlined **[5]**

(a) Transport of water, Active transport, Imbibition, Osmosis, Passive transport

(b) Right atrium, left ventricle, Right ventricle, Left atrium

(c) Sclera, Ciliary body, Cornea, Retina.

(d) Luteal phase, follicular phase, menstrual phase, ovulatory phase

(e) Vagina, ovary, uterus, oviduct, cervix (pathway of an egg after ovulation)

(iii) Match the items given in Column I with the most appropriate ones in Column II and rewrite the correct matching pairs. **[5]**

Column-I	Column-II
Auxin	Regulate Ovulation
Prolactin	Apical dominancy
LH	Milk production producer's
Green plants	Cell division
Cytokinin	Photolysis of water

(iv) Choose the odd one out from the following terms and name the category to which the others belong: **[5]**

(a) Sewage, Newspaper, Styrofoam, Hay

(b) Cretinism, Myxoedema, Simple goiter, Acromegaly

(c) Oxytocin, Insulin, Prolactin, Progesterone

(d) Auxin, Gibberellin, Cyton, Ethylene

(e) Light, CO2, H2O, N2

(v) State the exact location of the following structures: **[5]**

(a) Hypothalamus

(b) Glomerulus

(c) Retina

(d) Prostate gland

(e) Histone protein

Section B

(Attempt any four questions from this Section.)

Question 3.

(i) Define Transpiration **[1]**

(ii) Write down the difference between the following pairs as indicated within the brackets. Erythrocytes and leucocytes (function). **[2]**

(iii) Give reasons as to why gametes have a haploid number of chromosomes. **[2]**

(iv) Why are some substances biodegradable and others non-biodegradable? **[2]**

(v) The figure given below represents a stage during mitotic cell division in an animal cell: [3]

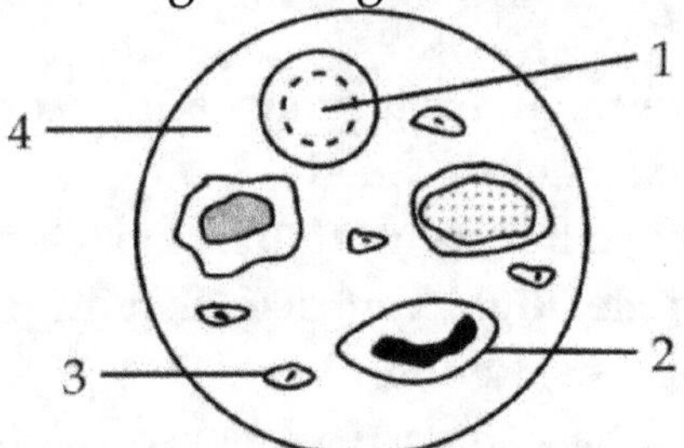

(a) Identify the stage, Give a reason to support your answer.
(b) Name the parts labelled 1,2 and 3.
(c) What is the chromosome number of the cell?
(d) Draw a neat labelled diagram of the cell as it would appear in the next stage. Name the stage.
(e) Mention where in the body this type of cell division occurs.

Question 4.

(i) Expand the abbreviation -NADPH [1]
(ii) Name the biodegradable pollutant [2]
(iii) Why do raisins swell up in the water? Explain by giving suitable reasons [2]
(iv) What is a placenta? Name the fetal and maternal components of the placenta. [2]
(v) Study the following diagram carefully and then answer the questions that follow. The diagram is depicting a defect of the human eye: [3]

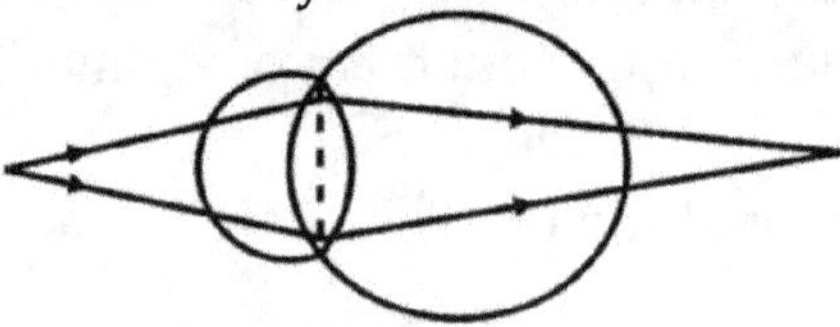

(a) Identify the defect shown in the diagram.
(b) Give two possible reasons for the above defect.
(c) Draw a neat labelled diagram to show how the above defect can be rectified.

Question 5.

(i) Define - Blood clotting [1]
(ii) What is the significance of synapse? [2]
(iii) State two functions of Aqueous humor [2]
(iv) A reflex arc in man is best described as a movement of stimuli from [2]
(v) Draw a neat and labeled diagram of the Malpighian Capsule. [2]

Question 6.

(i) Define -Autosomes [2]
(ii) Differentiate between near vision and distant vision (shape of the eye lens). [2]
(iii) State the function of photosensitive pigment present in the cone cells of the retina. [2]
(iv) Explain sex-linked disorders. [2]

(v) The diagram below represents a surgical steriliza tion method in males. Study the same an answer the questions that follow: **[3]**

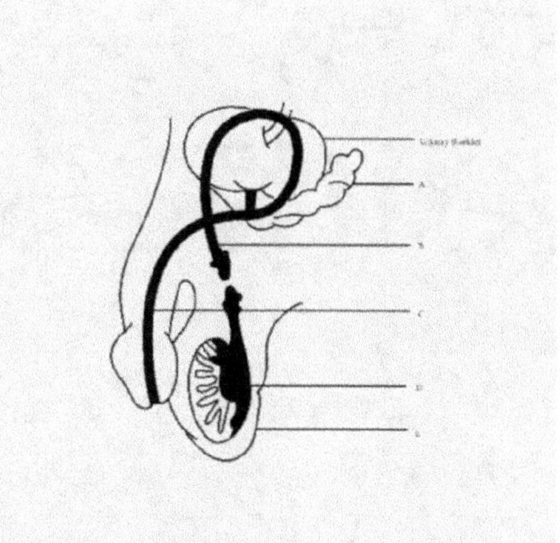

(a) Name the parts marked A, B, C, D and E.

(b) Give the name of the surgical method represented in the diagram.

(c) Which part is ligated or cut?

(d) Name the corresponding surgical method conducted in females.

(e) Name the part which ligated in females and why?

Question 7.

(i) Define Pollution **[1]**

(ii) Briefly explain the term reflex action. **[2]**

(iii) Difference between the Bowman's capsule and Malpighian capsule: **[2]**

(iv) What is environmental pollution? Write any two causes of pollution. **[2]**

(v) Draw a neat labeled diagram showing the cross sections of a root during water conduction. **[3]**

Question 8.

(i) Define -Turgor pressure **[2]**

(ii) What would you observe if a pot with a leafless shoot is kept under the jar? **[2]**

(iii) What is the difference between Chromosome and chromatid **[2]**

(iv) Explain the disease which is due to blood clotting. **[2]**

(v) Which structure will contain urine? **[3]**

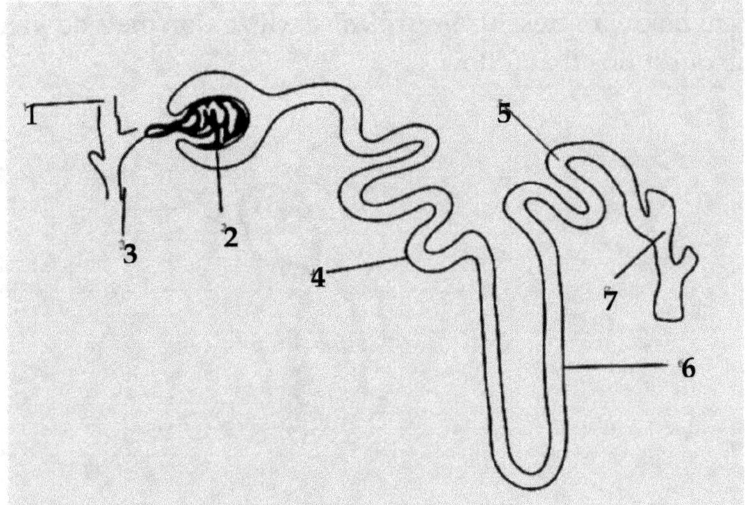

(a) The pigment that provides colour to urine.

(b) The process of removing excretory products from the body by artificial means.

ICSE 2023 EXAMINATION

SAMPLE TEST PAPER-4

BIOLOGY

(SCIENCE PAPER-2)

Maximum Marks: 80

Time allowed: Two hours

Answers to this Paper must be written on the paper provided separately.

You will not be allowed to write during first 15 minutes.

This time is to be spent in reading the question paper.

The time given at the head of this Paper is the time allowed for writing the answers.

(Section A is compulsory. Attempt any four questions from Section B.

The intended marks for questions or parts of questions are given in brackets [ ].

Section A

Answer all the questions from this section

Question 1. **[15]**

(i) The term "chromosomes" literally means

(a) Inherited bodies

(b) Twisted threads

(c) Coloured bodies

(d) Shining threads

Answer(c) Coloured bodies

(ii) The most appropriate characteristic is a semi-permeable. membrane is that

(a) It has minute pores.

(b) It has no pores.

(c) It allows the solute to pass through but not the solvent.

(d) It allows a solvent to pass through freely but Prevents the passage of the solute.

Answer(d) It allows a solvent to pass through freely but Prevents the passage of the solute.

(iii) With a decrease in atmospheric pressure, the rate of transpiration will

(a) Increase

(b) Decrease rapidly

(c) Decrease slowly

(d) Remain the same

Answer(a) Increase

(iv) The production of starch, and not glucose, is often used as a measure of photosynthesis in leaves because

(a) starch is the immediate product of photosynthesis.

(b) Glucose formed in photosynthesis soon gets Converted into starch.

(c) Starch is soluble in water.

(d) Sugar cannot be tested.

Answer(b) Glucose formed in photosynthesis soon gets Converted into starch.

(v) Granulocytes are :

(a) Lymphocytes and monocytes

(b) Lymphocytes and basophils

(c) Eosinophils and basophils

(d) Eosinophils and monocytes

Answer(c) Eosinophils and basophils

(vi) The pulse wave is caused by the

(a) Systole of the atria

(b) Diastole of the atria

(c) Systole of the left ventricle

(d) Systole of the right ventricle

Answer(c) Systole of the left ventricle

(vii) Excretion primarily involves

(a) Removal of all byproducts during catabolism.

(b) Removal of byproducts during anabolism.

(c) Removal of nitrogenous wastes.

(d) Throwing out excess water

Answer(c) Removal of nitrogenous wastes.

(viii) The insulating sheath covering the neural axon is called

(a) Plasmalemma

(b) Neurolemma

(c) Dura mater

(d) Pia mater

Answer(b) Neurolemma

(ix) On which day of the menstrual cycle does ovulation take place?

(a) 1st day

(b) 5th day

(c) 14th day

(d) 28th day

Answer(c) 14th day

(x) In females, how much time after fertilisation, does the fertilised egg get implanted in the uterine wall?

(a) Few months

(b) One month

(c) Three weeks

(d) About seven days in the flow of water into the cell.
Answer(d) About seven days in the flow of water into the cell.

(xi) A fully distended cell due to the absorption of water is called
(a) Flaccid.
(b) Both (a) and (b).
(c) Turgid.
(d) None of these.
Answer(c) Turgid.

(xii) Active transport is in a direction opposite to that of
(a) Osmosis
(b) Diffusion
(c) Neither (a) and (b)
(d) Both (a) and (b)
Answer(b) Diffusion

(xiii) Melting of glaciers takes place because of
(a) Eutrophication.
(b) Ozone depletion.
(c) Global warming.
(d) Acid rain.
Answer(c) Global warming.

(xiv) The inability to see in the diffused light is due to .
(a) Glaucoma.
(b) Cones.
(c) Rhodopsin.
(d) All of these
Answer(a) Glaucoma.

(xv) Which one is a plant harmone?
(a) Oxytocin
(b) Rhodopsin
(c) Cytokinin and Ethylene
(d) Cytosine
Answer(c) Cytokinin and Ethylene

Question 2.

(i) Name the following: **[5]**
(a) Rate of transpiration measured by
(b) Urine is formed by the kidneys by the combination of the following three processes.

(c) Capillaries are made up of.
(d) Protective membranes covering the human brain and spinal cord.
(e) A gaseous pollutant.

Answer

(a) Potometer
(b) • Glamerulus filteration
- Reabsorption
- Secretion

(c) Squamous endothelial cell
(d) Meninges
(e) SO_2

(ii) Arrange and rewrite the terms in each group in the correct order to be in a logical sequence beginning with the term that is underlined. **[5]**

(a) Pupil eye lens, vitreous humor, fovea centralis auditory nerve.
(b) Receptor, Spinal cord, Effector, Motor neuron, Sensory neuron.
(c) Pulmonary artery, Superior vena cava, Right ventricle, Lungs.
(d) The anterior lobe of the pituitary, Adrenocorticotropin
(e) Cortical cells, Root hair, xylem, Soil water, endodermis

Answer

(a) 1,2,3,4,5
(b) 1,3,5,4,2
(c) 3,1,2,4
(d) 3,2,5,1,4

(iii) Match the items given in Column I with the most appropriate ones in Column II and rewrite the correct matching pairs. **[5]**

Column I	Column II
(a) Demography	i Natality
(b) Liquid part of the blood without corpuscles	ii Regulate amount of water excreted
(c) ADH	iii Study of population
(d) Menopause	iv plasma
(e) Birth rate	v Complete stopage of Menstrual cycle

Answer

(a) iv
(b) v
(c) ii
(d) vi
(e) i

(iv) Choose the odd one out from the following terms and name the category to which the others belong: **[5]**

(a) Bile pigments, water, excretion, CO_2, urea.

(b) Xylem, epidermis, Wrinkled, cortex.

(c) Hypertonic, hypotonic, girdling, Isotonic.

(d) Anvil, Auxin, stirrup, oval window, Cochlea.

(e) Epididymis, scrotum, cervix, testis

Answer

(a) CO_2

(b) Wrinked

(c) Gridling

(d) Auxin

(e) Cervix

(v) State the exact location of the following structures: **[5]**

(a) Choroid

(b) Auxin

(c) Hammer

(d) Cortex

(e) Papillary muscle

Answer

(a) Between the selera and Retina

(b) At the aplical end of Root & shoot

(c) Attach the eardeum

(d) On top of your cerebrum

(e) With in the cavity of ventricles

Section B

(Attempt any four questions from this Section.)

Question 3.

(i) Define-Chordae tendinae. **[1]**

(ii) Differentiate between primary and accessory reproductive organs. **[2]**

(iii) What is the idea behind the phrase "population explosion"? **[2]**

(iv) What are nucleosomes? **[2]**

(v) The diagram given below represents the human Heart? in one phase of its functional activities. **[3]**

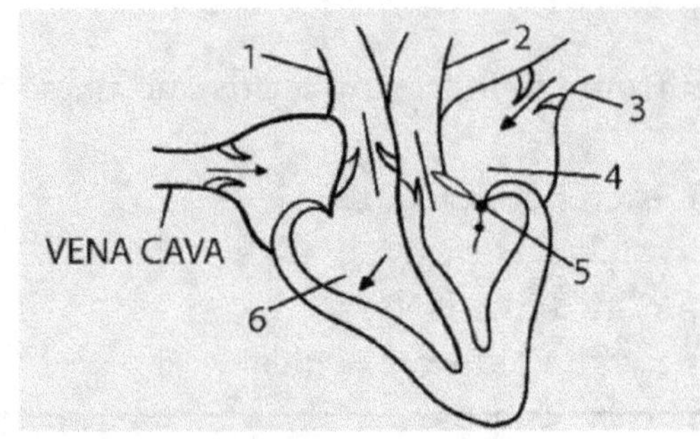

Study the sam. and answer the questions that follow:

(a) Name the phase.

(b) Label the parts 1,2 , and 3

(c) Which part of the heart is contracting in this phase,?

Give a reason to support your answer.

Question 4.

(i) Expand the abbreviation - RNA **[1]**

(ii) List any four traits in humans which you can easily study just by observing and making family charts. **[2]**

(iii) The cellophane paper has acted as a selectively or differentially permeable membrane. explain by giving suitable reasons. **[2]**

(iv) Turgor pressure helps to push through the hard ground. Explain **[2]**

(v) Given below is a diagram representing a stage during mitotic cell division in an animal cell. **[3]**

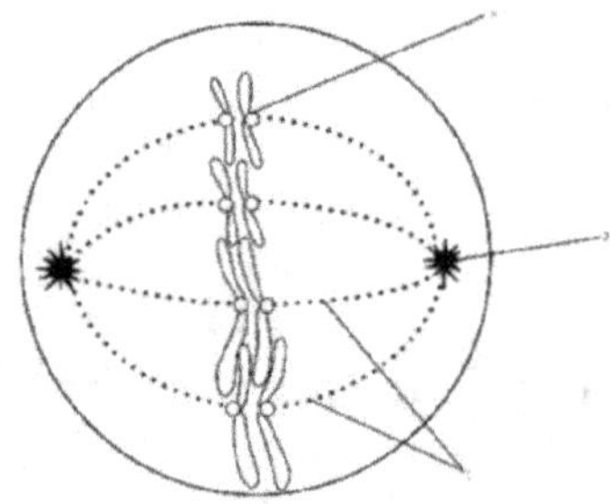

(a) Identify the above stage. Give a reason to support your answer.

(b) Name the cell organelle that forms the 'aster'.

(c) Name the part labbelled 1,2 and 3.

(d) Name the stage that follows this stage of mitosis. How can this stage be identified?

Question 5.

(i) Define-Thylakoids **[1]**

(ii) What are the main steps in the coagulation of blood? **[2]**

(iii) State two functions of association neurons. [2]
(iv) Why do you call the spinal cord and the brain a the central nervous system? [2]
(v) Draw a neat labeled diagram depicting a defect of the human eye. [3]

Question 6.

(i) Define -Eustachian tube [1]
(ii) Differentiate between Dynamic balance and static balance. [2]
(iii) State the function of the placenta with a suitable example. [2]
(iv) Carbon dioxide and urea, excreted by the fetus, removed? Explain. [2]
(v) The diagram given below refers to the vertical section of the eye of a mammal. Label the parts 1 to 10 to which the guideline points. [3]

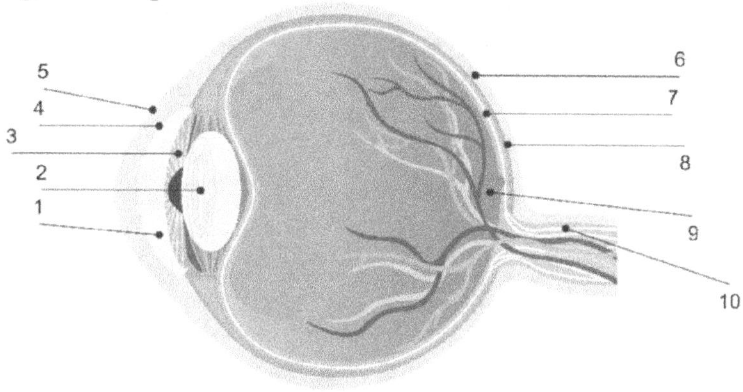

5
4
3
2
1
6
7
8
9
10

Question 7.

(i) Explain -SA Node. [1]
(ii) Give reasons why an alcoholic person drunk generally walks clumsily. [2]
(iii) Name two growth inhibitors plant hormone [2]
(iv) State one effect of each of Auxin and cytokinin [2]
(v) Draw a neat labeled diagram of a cross-section of Artery and vein [3]

Question 8.

(i) Name the process of transformation of several glucose molecules into one molecule of starch.[1]
(ii) Give two advantages of transpiration [2]
(iii) Mention one function of the following [2]
Lymphocytes, Thrombocytes.
(iv) A mature mammalian erythrocyte lacks a nucleus and mitochondria but is efficient in its functioning explain by giving a suitable reason. [2]
(v) Given alongside is a diagramatic sketch of a certain system in human body. [3]

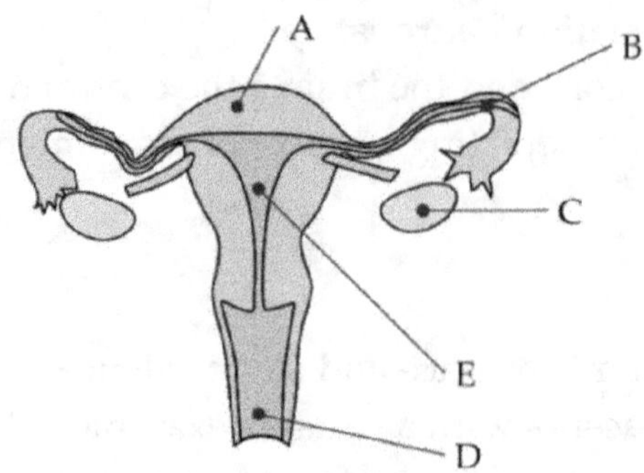

(a) Name the system,

(b) Name the parts labelled A, B, C and D.

(c) Part E represents a contraceptive device. What happens due to this device?

(d) Name the contraceptive method that could be applied in part B.

(e) In the method named in (d), is it required to be performed on both sides or just one side is enough ? Give reason.

ICSE 2023 EXAMINATION

SAMPLE TEST PAPER-5

BIOLOGY

(SCIENCE PAPER-2)

Maximum Marks: 80

Time allowed: Two hours

Answers to this Paper must be written on the paper provided separately.

You will not be allowed to write during first 15 minutes.

This time is to be spent in reading the question paper.

The time given at the head of this Paper is the time allowed for writing the answers.

(Section A is compulsory. Attempt any four questions from Section B.
The intended marks for questions or parts of questions are given in brackets [ ].

Section A

Answer all the questions from this section

Question 1. **[15]**

(i) Which of the following is the important function of emergency hormones?

(a) Decreases blood pressure and heart rate when the body is under stress.

(b) Increases blood pressure and heart rate when the body is in normal condition.

(c) Increases blood pressure and digestion when the body is under stress.

(d) Increases blood pressure and heart rate when the body is under stress.

Answer(d) Increases blood pressure and heart rate when the body is under stress.

(ii) What is the average length of a kidney in a human adult?

(a) 1 – 3 cm

(b) 5 cm

(c) 10 – 13 cm

(d) 20 cm

Answer(c) 10 – 13 cm

(iii) Blood vessels are:

(a) Coiled structure

(b) Branched structure

(c) Bifurcated structure

(d) Unbranched structure

Answer(b) Branched structure

(iv) The Pulse wave is mainly caused by the

(a) Systole of atria

(b) Diastole of atria

(c) Systole of the left ventricle

(d) Systole of the right ventricle

Answer(c) Systole of the left ventricle

(v) One of the examples of radiation pollutants is
(a) Sulphur dioxide
(b) Ozone
(c) Iodine 131
(d) Discarded fused electric bulbs
Answer(b) Ozone

(vi) Birth rate is the number of live births
(a) Per 1000 people per year
(b) Per 100 people per decade
(c) Per 1000 people per decade
(d) Per 100 people per year
Answer(c) Per 1000 people per year

(vii) The normal gestation period in humans is :
(a) 270 days
(b) 290 days
(c) 280 days
(d) 295 days
Answer(c) 280 days

(viii) The region in the eye where the rods and cones are located is the
(a) Retina
(b) Cornea
(c) Choroid
(d) Sclera
Answer(a) Retina

(ix) A mixed nerve is one which
(a) Carries sensations from 2 or more different sense organs.
(b) Contains both sensory and motor fibres.
(c) Has a common root but branches into two or more nerves to different organs.
(d) Has two or more roots from different parts of the brain.
Answer(b) Contains both sensory and motor fibres.

(x) Which one of the following in the real sense is NOT an excretory activity?
(a) Giving out carbon dioxide
(b) Passing out fecal matter
(c) Sweating
(d) Removal of urea.
Answer(b) Passing out fecal matter

(xi) Heart sounds are produced due to

(a) Closure of tricuspid and bicuspid valves

(b) Closure of aortic and pulmonary valves

(c) Rushing of blood through valves producing Turbulence

(d) Entry of blood into auricles

Answer(b) Closure of tricuspid and bicuspid valves

(xii) Which one chemical reaction occurs during photosynthesis?

(a) Carbon dioxide is reduced and water is oxidized.

(b) Water is reduced and carbon dioxide is oxidized.

(c) Both carbon dioxide and water are oxidized.

(d) Both carbon dioxide and water are reduced.

Answer(a) Carbon dioxide is reduced and water is oxidized.

(xiii) Transpiration will be fastest when the day is

(a) Cool, humid and windy

(b) Hot, humid and still

(c) Hot, humid and windy

(d) Hot, dry, and windy

Answer(d) Hot, dry, and windy

(xiv) The most appropriate characteristic of a semi-permeable. membrane is that

(a) It has minute pores.

(b) It has no pores.

(c) It allows the solute to pass through but not the solvent.

(d) It allows a solvent to pass through freely but prevents the passage of the solute.

Answer(d) It allows a solvent to pass through freely but prevents the passage of the solute.

(xv) Which one of the following is the phenotypic monohybrid ratio in F, generation?

(a) 3: 1

(b) 1: 2: 1

(c) 2: 2

(d) 1: 3

Answer(a) 3:1

Question 2.

(i) Name the following: **[5]**

(a) Total absence of pigment in the skin.

(b) Pressure of the cell contents on the cell wall.

(c) Loss of water as droplets from the margins of certain leaves.

(d) The cells that initiate blood clotting.

(e) The most numerous kind of leucocytes.

Answer

(a) Vitiligo

(b) Wall pressure

(c) Guttation

(d) Thrompbocytes

(e) Neutrophils

(ii) Arrange and rewrite the terms in each group in the correct order so as to be in a logical sequence beginning with the term that is underlined. **[5]**

(a) Renal artery, urethra, ureter, kidney, urinary bladder.

(b) The cochlea, tympanum, auditory canal, ear ossicles, and oval window.

(c) Implantation, ovulation, childbirth, gestation, fertilization.

(d) Sperm, Urethra, Sperm duct, Epididymis

(e) Sensory neuron, Association neuron, To muscle or glands, Motor neuron.

Answer

(a) 1,5,3,2,4

(b) 5,2,1,3,4

(c) 3,1,5,4.2

(d) 1,4,3,2

(e) 4,3,1,2

(iii) Match the items given in Column I with the most appropriate ones in Column II and rewrite the correct matching pairs. **[5]**

Column I		Column II
(a) Cretinism	i	Swelling of face and hands
(b) Phloem	ii	Dwarfism and mental retardation myxodema
(c) DNA	iii	Downward flow of sap
(d) Bile pigment	iv	Macromolecule
(e) Amino acid	v	Miromolecule
	vi	Protein
	vii	Dead WBC and RBC
	viii	Dead RBC only
	ix	Dead WBC only

Answer

(a) ii

(b) iii

(c) iv

(d) viii

(e) vi

(iv) Choose the odd one out from the following terms and name the category to which the others belong: **[5]**

(a) Kidney, ureter, Amino acid, urea, Urethra

(b) Stem elongation, Gibberellins, seed growth, ABA

(c) Placenta, Nutrients, oxygen, Antibodies, Synapse

(d) Acid rain, global warming, Toxoid, ozone depletion

(e) Acrosome, sperm, Autosome, penis, Testis

Answer

(a) Amino acids

(b) ABA

(c) Synapse

(d) Toxoid

(e) Autosome

(v) State the exact location of the following structures: **[5]**

(a) Testis

(b) Eyeball

(c) Granum

(d) DNA

(e) Gene

Answer

(a) Inside the scortum

(b) Orbit

(c) inside the chloroplasts of plant cells

(d) Located in the cell nucleus and also chloroplast and mitochordria

(e) On chromosome

Section B

(Attempt any four questions from this Section)

Question 3.

(i) Define- Mutation **[1]**

(ii) Give one difference between chromatids and chromatin. **[2]**

(iii) What is apical dominance? Give one example. **[2]**

(iv) Explain the semiconservative mode of replication. **[2]**

(v) The figure given below represents the vertical section of a leaf: **[3]**

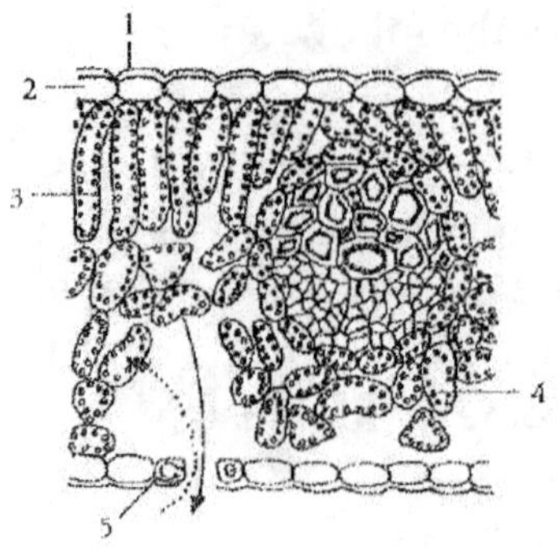

(a) Name the parts labelled 1 to 5

(b) What do the two arrows (dotted and solid) indicate in the day time and at night.

(c) Could you add one more arrow in the figure? I yes, what for?

(d) How many leaf veins have been shown in this section?

Question 4.

(i) Expand the abbreviation - AV Node

(ii) Name any two components which help in blood clotting

(iii) Salt solutions of different concentrations in relation to cells. Explain by giving suitable examples.

(iv) What is the purpose of the spring balance in the set-up during transpiration?

(v) Given alongside is a diagrammatic representation of a certain part of the process of circulation of blood in man. Study the same and then answer the questions that follow:

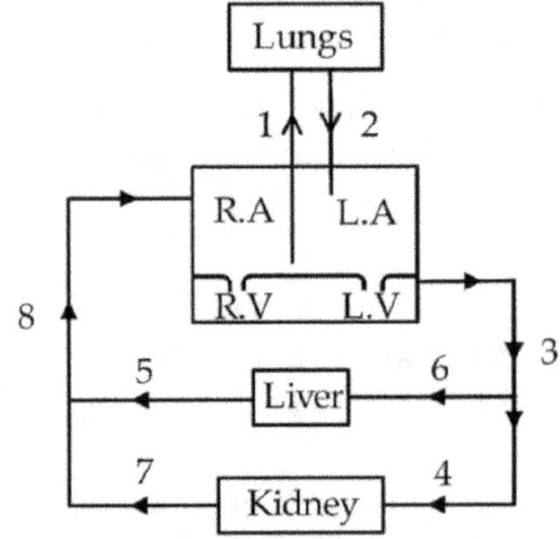

(a) Name the parts labelled 1,2,4 and 6 .

(b) Give the number and name of vessel which contains the maximum amount of urea a few hours after a protein rich meal.

(c) Draw a neat, labelled diagram of the 'cross-sectional' view of the blood vessel - numbered 3.

(d) Mention two structural difference between blood ves sels 3 and 8 .

Question 5.

(i) Define-color blindness **[1]**

(ii) Enumerate the structural differences between white blood cells and red blood cells. **[2]**

(iii) Mention two functions of the kidney. **[2]**

(iv) Mention the characteristics of the image that falls on the retina of the eye. **[2]**

(v) Draw a neat labeled diagram to show the internal structure of a human heart. **[3]**

Question 6.

(i) Define-systolic pressure **[1]**

(ii) Differentiate between Rod and Cones with reference to color differentiation. **[2]**

(iii) State the function of plant hormones with a suitable example. **[2]**

(iv) X-Linked disorders are generally seen in males. Explain with the help of a family chart. **[2]**

(v) Given below is an outline diagram of human body showing position of certain organs. **[3]**

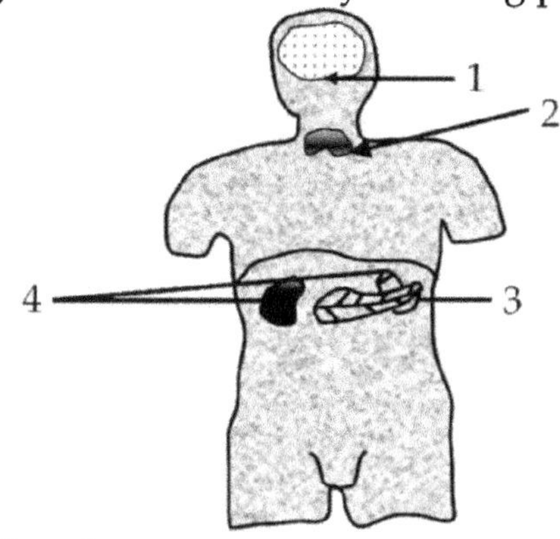

(a) Name the parts numbered 1 to 4.

(b) What is common to all these parts in regard to the nature of their functions?

(c) Name the nutrient element which is essential for the normal working of part 2.

Question 7.

(i) Explain - Photosynthesis **[1]**

(ii) Give reasons for how the rate of transpiration is affected by the humidity of the atmosphere. **[2]**

(iii) Differentiate between the cerebrum and spinal cord with respect to the arrangement of cytons and axons of neurons. **[2]**

(iv) State how sunlight affects transpiration. **[2]**

(v) Draw a neat labeled diagram of the Guard cell that shows the opening and closing of the stomata. **[3]**

Question 8.

(i) Define-XX and XY **[1]**

(ii) "Grapes shrink when immersed in a very strong sugar solution." Explain. **[2]**

(iii) What is the difference between temporary and permanent wilting? **[2]**

(iv) Explain two reasons for the high birth rate in India. **[2]**

(v) Given below is a diagram of a smear of human blood. Study the same and answer the questions that follow: **[3]**

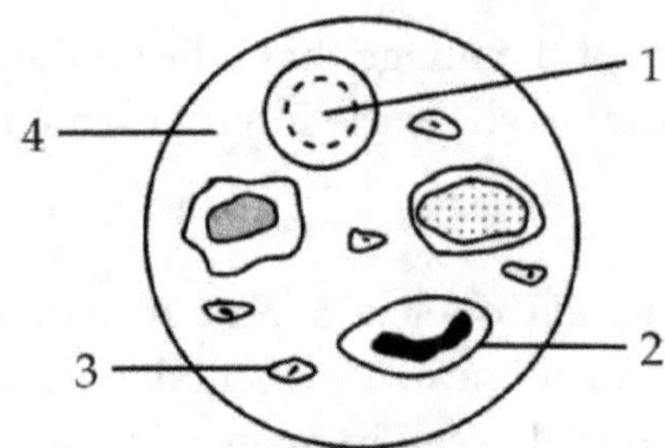

(a) Name the parts 12,3 and 4 indicated by guidelines.

(b) Mention two structural differences between the parts labelled I and 2.

(c) What is the main function of parts labelled 1,2 and 3 ?

(d) What is the life span of the part labelled 1?

(e) Name the soluble protein found in 4 which help in the clotting of blood

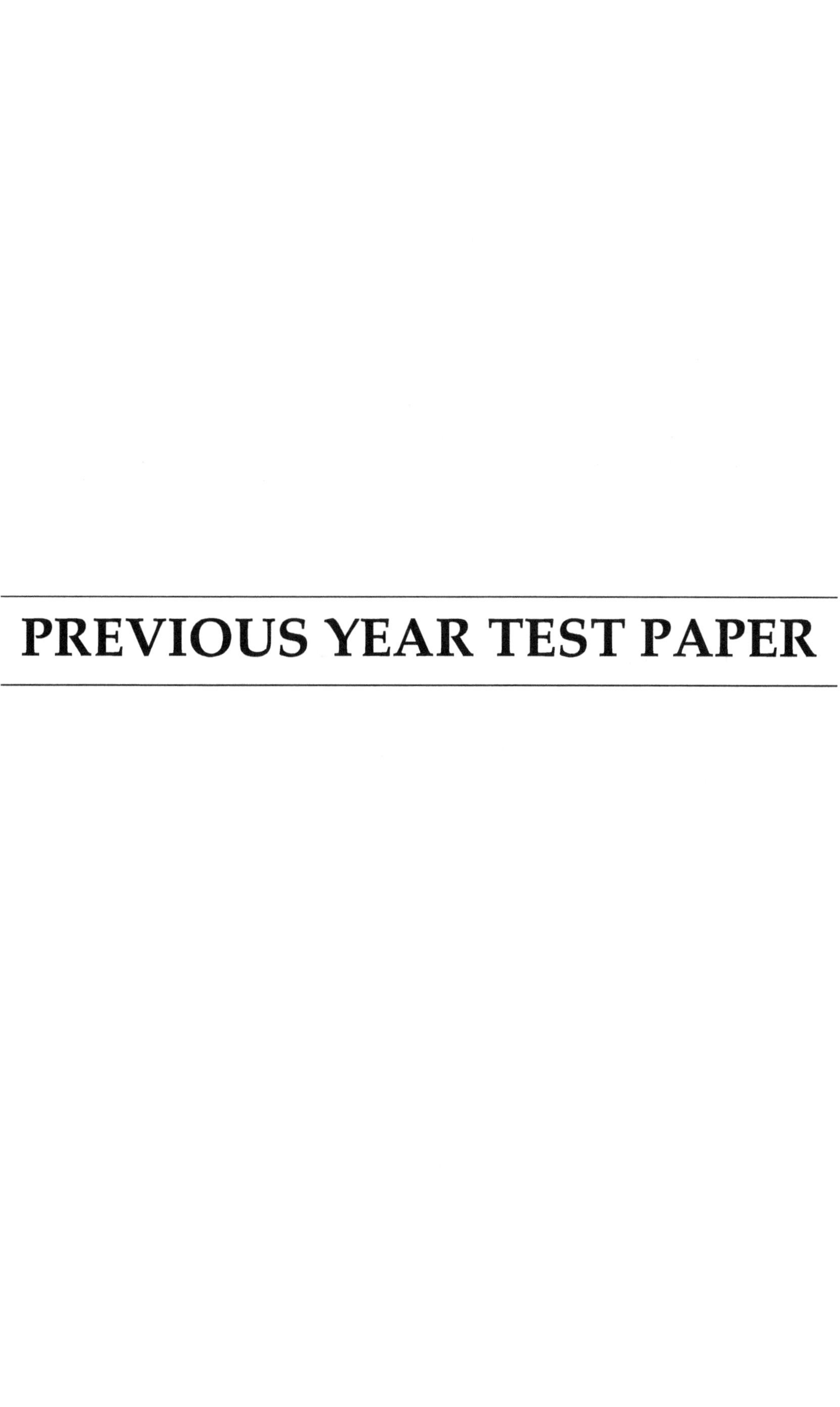

PREVIOUS YEAR TEST PAPER

ICSE 2019 EXAMINATION

PREVIOUS YEAR PAPER-**2019**

BIOLOGY

(SCIENCE PAPER-2)

Maximum Marks: 80

Time allowed: Two hours

Answers to this Paper must be written on the paper provided separately.

You will not be allowed to write during first 15 minutes.

This time is to be spent in reading the question paper.

The time given at the head of this Paper is the time allowed for writing the answers.

(Section A is compulsory. Attempt any four questions from Section B.

The intended marks for questions or parts of questions are given in brackets [ ].

Section A

Answer all the questions from this section

Question 1.

(i) Name the following: [5]

(a) The layer of the eyeball that provides nourishment to the eye.

Answer: choroid

(b) One gaseous compound which depletes the ozone layer.

Answer: Chloro fluoro carbons

(c) The structure which connects the placenta and the foetus.

Answer: umbilical chord

(d) A pair of corresponding chromosomes of the same shape and size and derived one from each parent.

Answer: Homologous chromosome

(e) The compound formed when hemoglobin combines with carbon dioxide in blood.

Answer: Carbamino hemoglobin

(ii) Correct and rewrite the statements by changing the biological term that is underlined for each statement. **[5]**

(a) The theory of inheritance of acquired characters was proposed by Watson and Crick.

Answer: The theory of inheritance of acquired characters was proposed By J.B.Lamarck.

(b) The protective sac which develops around the developing embryo is called the pericardium.

Answer: The protective sac which develops around the developing embryo is called the amniotic sac

(c) Maintaining balance of the body and coordinating muscular activities is carried out by the cerebrum.

Answer: Maintaining balance of the body and coordinating muscular activities is carried out by the Cerebellum.

(d) The kidney is composed of a number of neurons.

Answer: The kidney is composed of a number of nephrons.

(e) The part of the eye which can be donated from a clinically dead person is the retina.

Answer: The part of the eye which can be donated from a clinically dead person is the cornea.

(iii) Give suitable biological reasons for the following statements: **[5]**

(a) The birth rate in India is very high.

Answer: Indifferent attitude in birth controlling device .Early marriage, illiteracy are some of the causes of high birth rate in India. The people of rural area are unaware of the need of family planning.

(b) Carbon monoxide is dangerous when inhaled.

Answer: Inhaling too much of carbon monoxide is poisonous.

(c) Root hairs become flaccid and droop when excess fertilizers are added to the moist soil around them.

Answer: In outside soil there is more concentration of solutes due to the presence of fertilizers so water moves from the root hairs cells to the soil through the process of osmosis and root hair becomes flaccid.

(d) Acid rain is harmful to the environment.

Answer: Acid rain causes damage to building and monument. It increases acidity of soil. It causes neurological diseases.

(e) All life on Earth is supported by photosynthesis.

Answer: Green plants and some other organism prepare food in presence of sunlight and carbon dioxide by process of photosynthesis. All animals take food from plants and other animals. All animals depend on plants for food to obtain energy.

(iv) Match the items given in Column A with the most appropriate ones in Column B and rewrite the correct matching pairs. **[5]**

Column A	**Column B**
Cranial nerves	Testosterone
Leydig Cells	Natural Reflex
Acetylcholine	12 Pairs
Spinal Nerves	Prolactin

Sneezing	Neurotransmitter
	18 pairs
	31Pairs
	Conditioned reflex

Answer

Column A	Column B
Cranial nerves	12 pairs
Leydig Cells	Testosterone
Acetylcholine	Neurotransmitter
Spinal Nerves	31 pairs
Sneezing	Natural reflex

(v) Choose the correct answer from the four options given below: **[5]**

i While recording the pulse rate, where exactly does a doctor press on our wrist?

(a) Nerve
(b) Vein
(c) Artery
(d) Capillary

Answer: Artery

ii In a human male, a sperm will contain

(a) Both X and Y chromosomes
(b) Only Y chromosome
(c) Only X chromosome
(d) Either X or Y chromosome

Answer: Both X and Y chromosome

iii A muscular wall is absent in

(a) Capillary
(b) Venule
(c) Arteriole
(d) Vein

Answer: Capillary

iv On which day of the menstrual cycle does ovulation take place?

(a) 5th day
(b) 28th day
(c) 14th day
(d) 1st day

Answer: 14th day

v Which one of the following does not affect the rate of transpiration?

(a) Light
(b) Humidity
(c) Wind
(d) Age of the plant

Answer: Age of Plant

(vi) Identify the ODD term in each set and name the CATEGORY in which the remaining of these belong: **[5]**

Example: Glucose, starch, cellulose, calcium

Odd term: Calcium Category: Others are different types of carbohydrates.

(a) Addison's disease, Cushing's Syndrome, Acromegaly, Leukemia

Answer: Leukimia is a cancer of blood cells while the other three are endocrinal disorder.

(b) Insulin, Adrenaline, Pepsin, Thyroxine

Answer: pepsin is not seretedby endocrine glands.

(c) Axon, Dendron, Photon, Cyton

Answer: Axon ,Dendron,cyton are part of neuron while photon is a light particle.

(d) Chicken pox, Colour blindness, Haemophilia, Albinism

Answer: Colour Blindness, Haemophilia, albenism are genetic disorder while chicken pox is a viral infection.

(e) Polythene bag, Crop residue, Animal waste, Decaying vegetable

Answer: Only polythene bag is non- biodegradable.

(vii) Expand the following biological abbreviations: **[5]**

(a) ABA –Abcisic acid

(b) IAA- Indole acetic acid

(c) ATP- adenosine triphosphate

(d) DNA- Deoxyribonucleic Acid

(e) TSH – Thyroid Stimulating Hormone

Study the picture given below and answer the following questions:

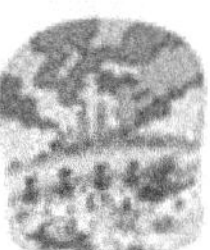

(i) Identify the type of pollution.

Answer: Water Pollution

(ii) Name one pollutant that causes the above pollution.

Answer: Industrial effluent

(iii) Mention the impact of this pollution on human health.
Answer: Large amount of Nitrates are dissolved in the water from industrial waste . It will contaminate the water and cause serious health hazards.

(iv) State one measure to control this pollution.
Answer: Factories should treat wastes before releasing into water bodies.

(v) What is a 'pollutant'? Explain the term
Answer: The substance as certain chemicals or waste that renders the normal properties of environment are called pollutant. They may be air pollutants, Water pollutant, soil pollutants.

Section B

Attempt any four questions from this section.

Question 2.

(i) Given below is an experimental setup to demonstrate a particular tropical movement in germinating seeds. Study the diagram and answer the questions that follows: **[5]**

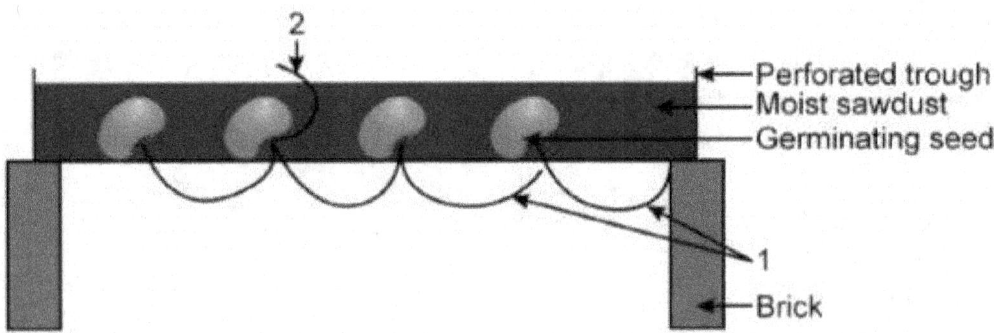

(a) Label the parts 1 and 2.
(b) Name the tropical movement shown in part 1.
(c) Part 1 is affected by two stimuli. Which one of the two is stronger?
(d) What is thigmotropism? Give one Example.
(e) What is meant by 'positive ' and 'negative 'tropic movement in plants?

Answer:

(a) Part 1 is radicle and part 2 is plumule.
(b) Geotropism is shown by Part-1.
(c) Stimulus of gravity and stimulus of water. Water is stronger stimulus than gravity.
(d) The growth and movements of plants in response to touch is called thigmotropism. These types of movements are seen in tendrils.Tendrils of sweat Pea, grapes when comes in contact with any support it coil around it.
(e) Positive tropic movement is the movement of a part of a plant when it grows towards a stimulus. Example: growth of stem towards light.

Negative tropic movement is the movement of a part of plant when it grows away from the stimulus. For Example –movement of root away from the light.

(ii) Mention the exact location of each of the following **[5]**

(a) Testis-

Testis are two oval shaped organs in the male reproductive system. They are contained in a sack of skin called scrotum.

(b) Incus-

The incus or anvil is a bone in the middle ear and joined to the stapes or stirrup bone.

(c) Thylakoids-

Chlorophyll is located in a concentrated form in the thylakoid membrane of organelles called chloroplasts.

(d) Amniotic fluid-

The amniotic fluid is the protective liquid contained by the amniotic sac of a gravid amniote. This fluid serves as a cushion for the growing fetus,

(e) Corpus callosum

Located near the center of the brain, the Corpus callosum is the largest bundle of nerve fibers that connects the left and right cerebral hemispheres.

Question 3.

(i) The diagram given below represents an experiment to prove the importance of a factor in photosynthesis. Answer the questions that follow. **[5]**

(a) Name the factor studied in the experiment.
(b) What will you observe in experimental leaf after the starch test?
(c) Explain the process of photosynthesis.
(d) Give a balanced chemical reaction to represent the process of photosynthesis.
(e) Draw a neat labeled diagram of experimental set-up to show that oxygen is released during photosynthesis

Answer:

(i) [5]

(a) Light is necessary for photosynthesis.

(b) The leaf turns blue black except in covered region which turn brown in colour. As this covered region did not receive light, photosynthesis did not occur and no starch is formed.

(iii) Balanced chemical reaction:

(c) iv) Photosynthesis is a biochemical process by which green plants synthesize their food in presence of carbon dioxide from atmosphere and water from soil inpresence of sun-light. Glucose is synthesized during the process which is converted into starch.

(d) Experimental setup to show that oxygen is released during photosynthesis.

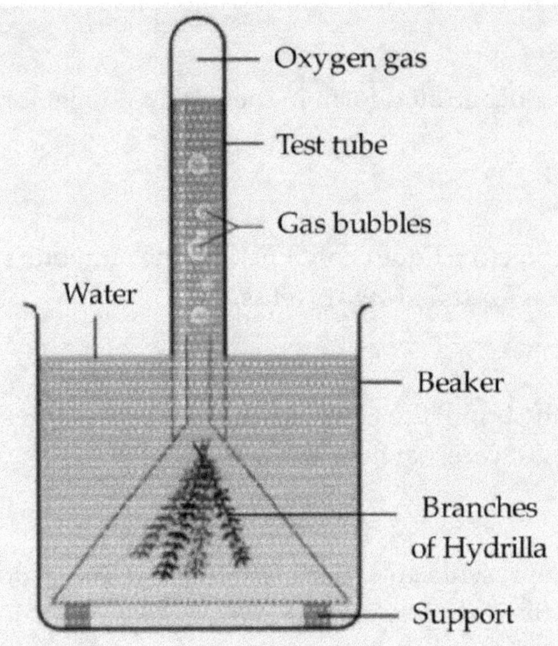

(ii) State the main function of the following: [5]

(a) Medulla Oblongata

(b) Cytokinins

(c) Tears

(d) Coronary Artery

(e) Seminal vesicles

Answer:

(a) Medulla oblongata-

Answer: The primary function of the medulla oblongata is to control autonomic functions throughout the body. It controls functions like heartbeat, breathing and digestion.

(b) Cytokinins –

Answer: these are plant growth substances that promote cell division and organ formation. It counter act apical dominance.

(c) Tears

Answer: Tears prevent dryness by coating the surface of the eye, as well as protect it from external irritation. Foreign bodies thatenters the eye are washed out by tears.

(d) Coronary artery

Answer: Coronary arteries supply blood to the heart muscle.

(e) Seminal vesicles –

Answer: The seminal vesicle is responsible for producing a milky fluid called semen. The thick fluid contains a mixture of substances, including citric acid, proteins, sugar fructose and potassium.

Question 4.

(i) The diagram given below represents an organ system in the human body. Study the same and answer the questions that follow: **[5]**

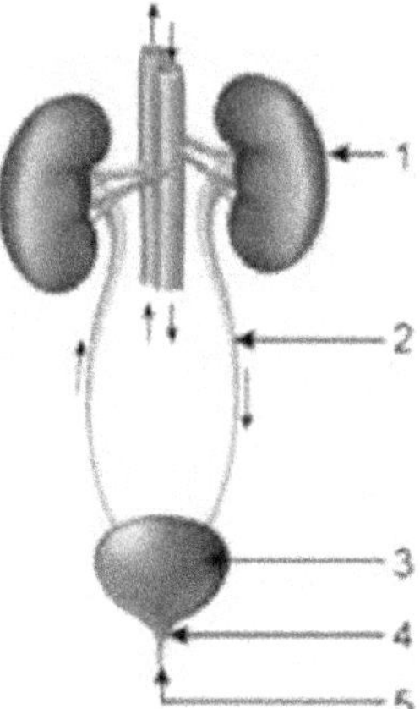

(a) Identify the system.
(b) Label the parts marked 2 - 4. Mention the function of part 5
(c) Name the structural and functional units of the part marked 1.
(d) What is the fluid that accumulates in part 3?
(e) Which is the main nitrogenous waste present in it?
(f) Draw a neat labelled diagram showing longitudinal section of part- 1.

Answer:

(a) Humanexcretory system
(b) Part 2 is Ureter and Part 4 is sphincter
(c) The urethra is a tube responsible for allowing urine to leave the body as it empties from the bladder.
(d) Nephron is the structural and functional unit of Part-1.
(e) Urine is the fluid that accumulates in part 3. It contains urea and creatinine.
(f) L. S .of Kidney

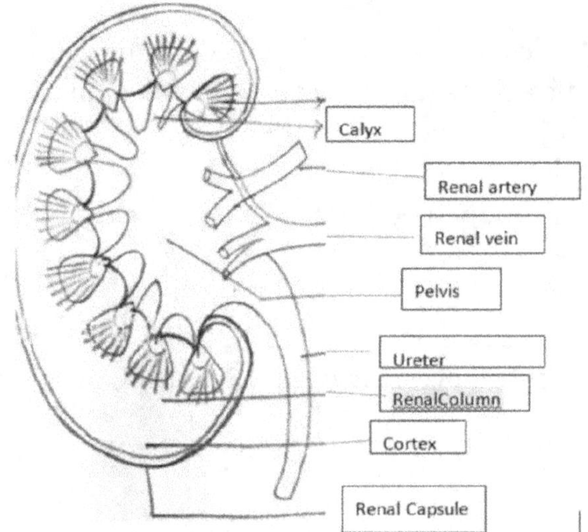

(ii) The diagram given below represents an endocrine gland in the human body. Study the diagram and answer the following questions: [5]

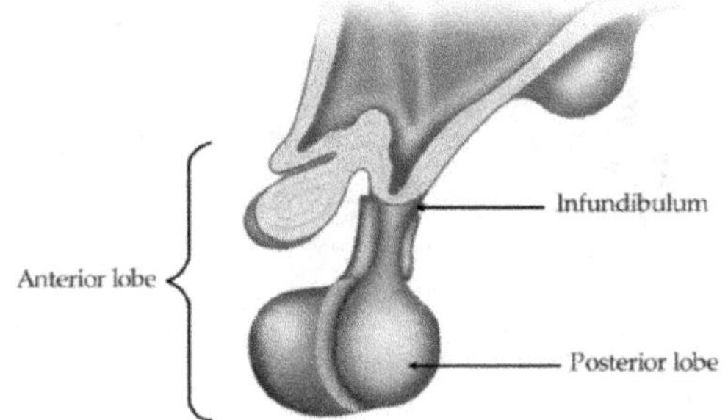

(a) Identify the endocrine gland. Where is it located?

(b) Why is the above gland referred to as the 'master gland'?

(c) Name the hormone which in deficiency causes diabetes insipidus. How does this disorder differ from diabetes mellitus?

(d) Explain the term 'hormone'. What is the role of tropic hormones in the human body?

(e) Which lobe of the above gland secretes

i. Oxytocin

ii. ACTH

iii. Growth Hormone

Answer:

(a) Pitutary Gland. The pituitary is a small gland located below the brain in the skull base below the hypothalamus.

(b) It is often called the "master gland" because it controls the functions of all other endocrine glands.

(c) Decrease secretion of Anti Diuretic Hormone causes diabetic Insipidus. Diabetic Mellitus is caused due to deficiency of Insulin hormone.

(d) A hormone is a biological compound used by multicellular organisms to organize, coordinate, and control the functions of their cells and tissues. A tropic hormone stimulates other endocrine gland to release their hormone.

(e) Oxytocin- Posterior pituitary lobe
ACTH-Anterior pituitary lobe
Growth hormone – Anterior pituitary lobe

Question 5.

(i) Given below is an apparatus which was set up to investigate a physiological process in plants. The set-up was placed in bright sunlight. Answer the questions that follow: [5]

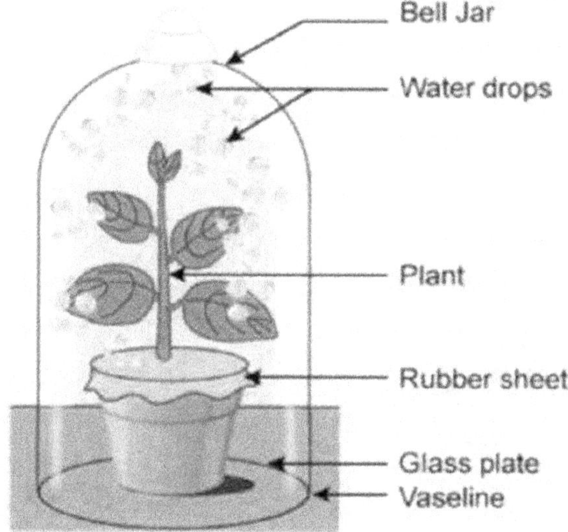

(a) Name the process being studied. Define the process.
(b) Why was the pot enclosed in a rubber sheet?
(c) Mention two external factors which can accelerate the above process.
(d) List two adaptations in plants to reduce the above process.
(e) Draw a neat labelled diagram of a stomatal apparatus.

Answer:

(i)

(a) Transpiration is taking place. The process by which plant loses water by the process of evaporation through stomata is called transpiration.
(b) The plastic bag is to prevent the escape of water vapour from the pot.
(c) Transpiration increases with increase in temperature. Wind increases the rate of transpiration. Sunlight also increases the rate of temperature.
(d) Thick cuticle on leaves reduced the loss of water by transpiration. Narrow leaves reduce the exposed surface area for transpiration. Fewer stomata reduce the rate of transpiration.

(e)

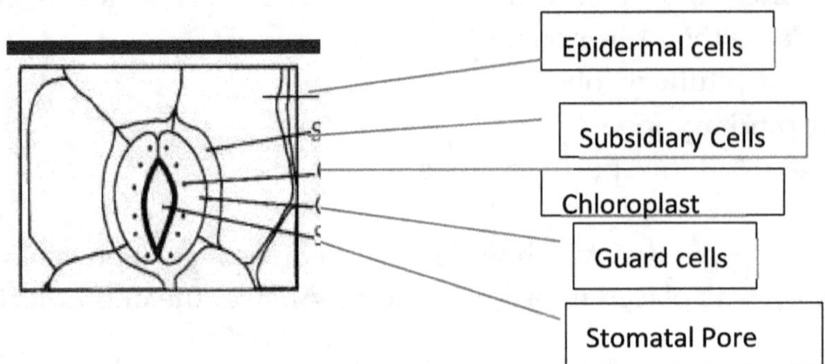

STOMATAL APERATUS

(ii) Given below are two stages in the evolution of man. Study them and answer the questions that follow: [5]

A.

B.

(a) Identify Australopithecus and Neanderthal man from the above pictures

(b) Mention two characteristic features each for the two stages.

(c) Who proposed the theory of 'natural selection'?

(d) Name the organism used as an example to explain 'industrial melanism'.

(e) Give two examples of vestigial organs in humans.

Answer:

(a) A is Neanderthal B is Australopithecus

(b) Characteristics feature of Australopithecus:

i. Members of Austrapithecus are a combination of human like and apelike traits.

ii. Distinct Lumbar curve was present in vertebral column.

Characteristics feature of Neanderthal.

i. Neanderthals walk upright with bipedal movement..

ii. The jaw was deep with no chin and skull bones were thick.

(c) Charle's Darwin proposed the theory of Natural Selection.

(d) The organism used as an example of Industrial Melanismoccurred in Peppered Moth, Biston Betularia.

(e) Vermiform Appendix , Wisdom Tooth

Question 6.

(i) In Mendel's experiments, tall pea plants (T) are dominant over dwarf pea plants (t). [5]

(a) What is the phenotype and genotype of the F1 generation if a homozygous tall plant is crossed with a homozygous dwarf plant?

(b) Draw a Punnett square board to show the gametes and offspring when both parents are heterozygous for tallness.

(c) What is the phenotypic and Genotypic ratioof above cross in(ii)

(d) State Mendel's Law of Dominance.

(e) What is a dihybrid cross?

Answer:

(i)

(a) Phenotypic Ratio -: tall genotypic ratio : Tt

	T	t
T	TT	Tt

(b)

t	Tt	tt

.

(c) Phenotypic Ratio 3 : 1 Genotypic Ratio 1: 2 : 1

(d) Mendel's Law of Dominance.

This when two alternating forms of traits or characters are present are present in an organism only one factor expresses itself in F1 progeny. The factor that expresses itself is called dominant factor and the other factor which remain hidden is called recessive factor.

(e) A dihybrid cross is a breeding experiment between parental generation organisms that differ in two traits.

(ii) Given below is a diagram representing a stage during mitotic cell division. Study the diagram and answer the following questions. [5]

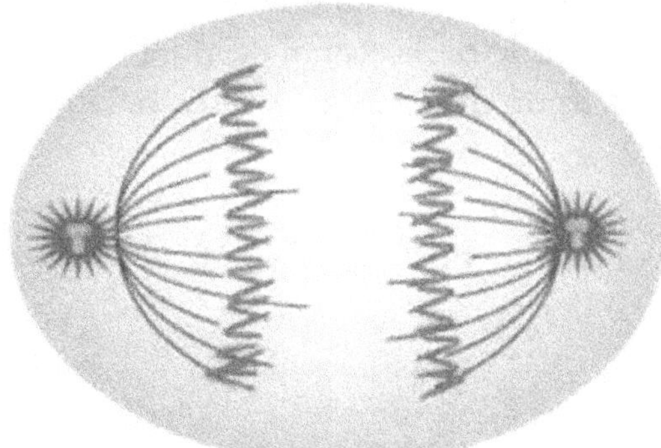

(a) Identify the stage by giving a suitable reason.

(b) Is it a plant or an animal cell?. Give a reason to support your answer.

(c) Draw a neat, labelled diagram of the stage which follows the one shown in the diagram.

(d) How many chromosomes will each daughter cell have after the completion of the above division?

(e) Name the four nitrogenous bases.

Answer:

(a) Two sister chromatids of each chromosome separate from each other and move to opposite poles so this is Anaphase.

(b) This is an Animal cell because centrioles are seen at the opposite poles.

(c) Telophase is followed by Anaphase.

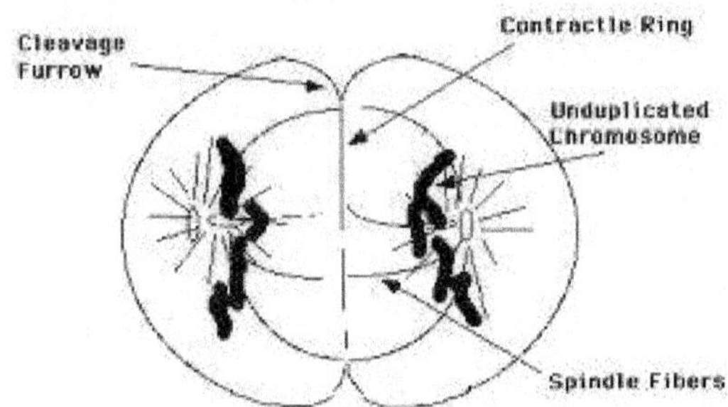

Telophase

(d) Each daughter cell will have one set of chromosome present in parent cell.

(e) Adenine, Guanine , cytosine ,thymine are four nitrogenous bases.

Question 7.

(i) Answer the following questions briefly

(a) How are cytons and axons placed in the brain and spinal cord?

Answer: The grey matter containing Cytonsis placed in the outer portion and the white matter containing axon id placed in the inner portion in the brain. In the spinal cord grey matter is placed on the inner portion and the white matter is placed on the outer portion.

(b) Which part of the Human ear gives 'Dynamic balance' and 'static balance' to the body?

Answer: The sensory cells in semicircular canal of inner ear gives dynamic equilibrium and the utriculus and sacculus cells of innerear give static balance.

(c) Explain how the human eye adapts itself to bright light and dim light.

Answer: The movements of muscle fibres of iris control the size of pupil and regulate the amount of light entering the light.

(d) What is parthenocarpy? Give one example.

Answer: The process of development of fruit without fertilization is called parthenocarpy. In fruits like apple, banana auxin induces fruit formation.

(e) Mention any two objectives of 'Swachh Bharat Abhiyaan'.

Answer: Objectives of 'Swachh Bharat Abhiyaan' are -

i. The first objective of the mission is to construct individual and community toilets.

ii. The other objective is to reduce or eliminate open defecation from the country. Open defecation results in the deaths of thousands of children every year due to unhygienic living conditions and diseases.

(ii) The diagram given below represents a system in the human body. Study the diagram and answer the following questions. [5]

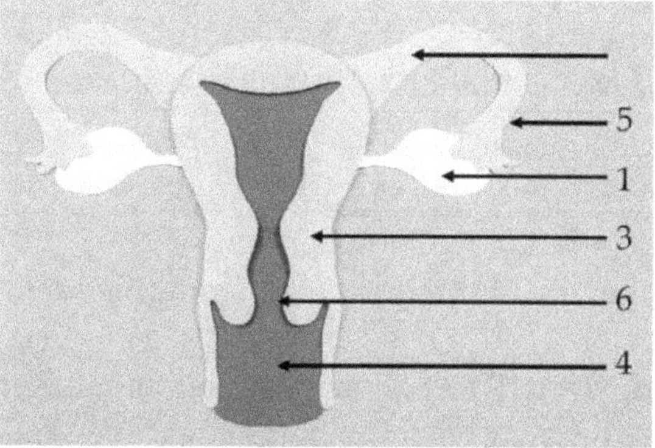

(a) Identify the system.

(b) Label the parts marked 5 and 6

(c) Name the two hormones secreted by 1.

(d) Mention the number and the name of the part involved in fertilization and implantation from the above diagram.

(e) Mention the surgical methods of contraception in 1

Answer:

(a) Female Reproductive System is shown in the given Diagram.

(b) Part 5 is Fallopian tube. Part 6 is cervix.

(c) Two hormone secreted by 1 are oestrogen and Progesterone.

(d) the number and the name of the part involved in fertilization and implantation from the above diagram

Process	Number	Name
Fertilization	2	Fallopian Tube
Implantation	3	Uterus

(e) Surgical methods of contraception in male is called Vasectomy and for female it is called tubectomy.

ICSE 2023 EXAMINATION
PREVIOUS YEAR PAPER-**2021**
BIOLOGY
(SCIENCE PAPER-2)

Maximum Marks: 40

Time allowed: Two hours

Answers to this Paper must be written on the paper provided separately.

You will not be allowed to write during first 15 minutes.

This time is to be spent in reading the question paper.

The time given at the head of this Paper is the time allowed for writing the answers.

(Section A is compulsory).

The intended marks for questions or parts of questions are given in brackets [ ].

Section A
Answer all the questions from this section

Question 1. **[15]**

(i) The process of conversion of ADP to ATP during photosynthesis:

(a) Polymerisation
(b) Photophosphorylation
(c) Photorespiration
(d) Photolysis

Answer: (b)

(ii) Permanently open structures seen on the barks of old woody stems:

(a) Stomata
(b) Hydathodes
(c) Lenticels
(d) Epidermal pores

Answer: (c)

(iii) The pressure developed in the roots due to continuous inward movement of water by cell-to-cell osmosis:

(a) Root Pressure
(b) Wall Pressure
(c) Turgor Pressure
(d) Air Pressure

Answer: (a)

(iv) The type of gene, which in presence of a contrasting allele is not expressed:

(a) Homozygous
(b) Heterozygous
(c) Dominant
(d) Recessive

Answer: (d)

(v) After mitosis, a female human cell will have:
(a) 44+XX chromosomes
(b) 22+X chromosomes
(c) 22+Y chromosomes
(d) 44+XY chromosomes
Answer: (a)

Question 2.

Complete the following statements by choosing the appropriate option for each blank: **[5]**

(i) At the end of _______________, cytokinesis is completed.
(a) Metaphase
(b) Prophase
(c) Interphase
(d) Telophase
Answer: (d)

(ii) The genotype of a person who cannot roll his tongue is ________________.
(a) Rr
(b) RR
(c) rr
(d) RRr
Answer: (c)

(iii) When a cell is placed in a ___________________ solution it becomes plasmolysis.
(a) Distilled water
(b) Hypertonic
(c) Isotonic
(d) Hypotonic
Answer: (b)

(iv) The nitrogenous base Adenine always pairs with _____________
(a) Thymine
(b) Guanine
(c) Cytosine
(d) Thiamine
Answer: (a)

(v) The basic units of heredity are ______________________
(a) Chromosomes
(b) Chromatids

(c) Genes
(d) Centrosome
Answer: (c)

Question 3.

Choose the correct answer from each of the four options given below: **[5]**

(i) NADP is expanded as:
(a) Nicotinamide Adenosine Dinucleotide Phosphate
(b) Nicotinamide Adenine Dinucleotide Phosphate
(c) Nicotinamide Adenine Dinucleolus Phosphate
(d) Nicotinamide Adenosine Dinucleolus Phosphate
Answer: (b)

(ii) Transpiration is useful to the plant because it:
(a) Creates a suction force for absorption of water from the soil
(b) Helps in photophosphorylation
(c) Synthesises glucose
(d) Splits water molecules
Answer: (a)

(iii) A homozygous pea plant having purple flowers is crossed with a homozygous pea plant bearing white flowers. The phenotypic ratio of the offspring obtained in F2 generation is:
(a) 2:1
(b) 1:1
(c) 1:2:1
(d) 3:1
Answer: (d)

(iv) The shoot from a balsam plant is kept in a beaker containing eosin solution (pink). The pink colour will be distinctly seen in the:
(a) Xylem
(b) Phloem
(c) Epidermis
(d) Cortex
Answer: (a)

(v) Replication of DNA in the cell cycle occurs during the:
(a) G1 – Phase
(b) Anaphase
(c) S – Phase
(d) G2 – Phase
Answer: (c)

Question 4.

Explain the following terms: **[5]**

(i) Karyokinesis

(a) It is the division of nucleus during cell division

(b) It is the division of cytoplasm during cell division

(c) It is the division of centrosome

(d) It is the division of nucleolus

Answer: (a)

(ii) Law of Dominance

(a) Out of a pair of contrasting alleles present together, only the recessive allele is able to express itself while the dominant remains suppressed

(b) Out of a pair of contrasting alleles present together, only the dominant allele is able to express itself while the recessive remains suppressed

(c) Out of a pair of contrasting alleles present together, both dominant and recessive cannot express themselves

(d) Out of a pair of contrasting alleles present together, both dominant and recessive can express themselves

Answer: (b)

(iii) Mutation:

(a) It is a sudden change in one or more genes in an organism's cells which is heritable

(b) It is a change in the number of centrosomes in an organism's cell which is heritable

(c) It is a change in the structure of cell membrane in an organism's cells which is heritable

(d) It is a change in the shape of cells which is heritable

Answer: (a)

(iv) Photosynthesis

(a) It is the synthesis of glucose from carbon dioxide by non-green plants using light energy.

(b) It is the synthesis of glucose by green plants from carbon dioxide using light energy.

(c) It is the synthesis of glucose from carbon dioxide and water by non-green plants using light energy.

(d) It is the synthesis of glucose from carbon dioxide and water by green plants using light energy.

Answer: (d)

(v) Transpiration:

(a) It is the loss of water in the form of droplets from the aerial parts of the plant.

(b) It is the loss of water in the form of water vapour from the underground parts of the plant.

(c) It is the loss of water in the form of water vapour from the aerial parts of the plant.

(d) It is the loss of water in the form of water vapour from all parts of the plant.
Answer: (c)

Question 5.

Mention the exact location of the following: **[5]**

(i) Aster

(a) Around the centrioles in plant cells
(b) Around the centrioles in animal cells
(c) Around the chromatids in animal cells
(d) Around the chromatids in plant cells
Answer: (b)

(ii) Guard cells

(a) Around the root hairs
(b) Around the lenticels
(c) Around the thylakoids
(d) Around the stoma
Answer: (d)

(iii) Xylem tissue:

(a) Conducts water and minerals in leaves
(b) Does not conduct water and minerals in stems
(c) Conducts food and nutrition to roots
(d) Conducts food and nutrients to all parts of the plant
Answer: (a)

(iv) Centrioles

(a) Found only in plant cells
(b) Found inside nucleus
(c) Found only in animal cells
(d) Found in animal and plant cells
Answer: (c)

(v) Genes

(a) Present on cell walls
(b) Present on chloroplast
(c) Present on chromosomes
(d) Present on centrosomes
Answer: (c)

Question 6.

State the function of the following: **[5]**

(i) Cell wall

(a) Regulates entry of solutes in plant cells

(b) Regulates entry of solutes in animal cells

(c) Gives rigidity and shape to plant cells

(d) Gives rigidity and shape to animal cells

Answer: (c)

(ii) Centromere:

(a) It is the point of attachment of two sister chromatids

(b) It is the point of attachment of two centrioles

(c) It is the point of attachment of two centrosomes

(d) It is the point of attachment between two daughter nuclei

Answer: (a)

(iii) Cuticle on leaves:

(a) Prevents photosynthesis

(b) Reduces transpiration

(c) Protects leaves from grazing animals

(d) Gives colour to leaves

Answer: (b)

(iv) Hydathodes

(a) Transpiration

(b) Absorption of water

(c) Photosynthesis

(d) Guttation

Answer: (d)

(v) Grana of chloroplast is not the:

(a) Site of Light Independent Phase

(b) Site of Light Dependent Phase

(c) Site of Photolysis

(d) Site of Photon Absorption

Answer: (a)

Question 7. **[5]**

The diagram given below presents an experiment to demonstrate a particular aspect of Photosynthesis. The letter 'A' indicates a certain condition inside the flask: Answer the Questions:

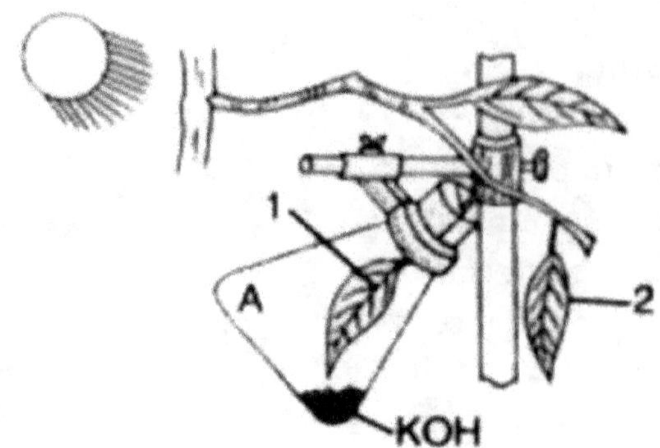

(i) What is the aim of the experiment?

(a) To show that oxygen is released during photosynthesis

(b) To show that photosynthesis occurs in the presence of KOH

(c) To show that chlorophyll is necessary for photosynthesis

(d) To show that carbon dioxide is necessary for photosynthesis

Answer: (d)

(ii) What is the special condition inside the flask?

(a) Air inside the flask is free of oxygen

(b) Air inside the flask is free of carbon dioxide

(c) Air inside the flask is free of nitrogen

(d) KOH purifies the air inside the flask

Answer: (b)

(iii) An alternative chemical that can be used instead of KOH is:

(a) Sodium Hydroxide

(b) Sodium Chloride

(c) Potassium Chloride

(d) Potassium Permanganate

Answer: (a)

(iv) In what manner, do the leaves 1 and 2 differ at the end of the starch test?

(a) Leaf 1 turns brown, Leaf 2 turns blue black

(b) Leaf 1 turns blue black, Leaf 2 turns blue brown

(c) Leaf 1 turns purple, Leaf 2 remains green

(d) There is no change in the colour of the leaves

Answer: (a)

(v) What is the important step that should be taken before performing this experiment?

(a) The plant should be placed in dark for 24 hours to destarch the entire plant.

(b) The plant should be placed in dark for 24 hours to remove chlorophyll from the leaves

(c) The plant should be placed in dark for 24 hours to destarch the leaves

(d) The plant should be placed in dark for 24 hours for the roots to absorb water

Answer: (c)

Question 8. **[5]**

Given below is the diagram of an experiment step-up to study the process of Transpiration. Cobalt chloride papers are fixed on the upper as well as lower surface of the leaf. Answer the question that follow:

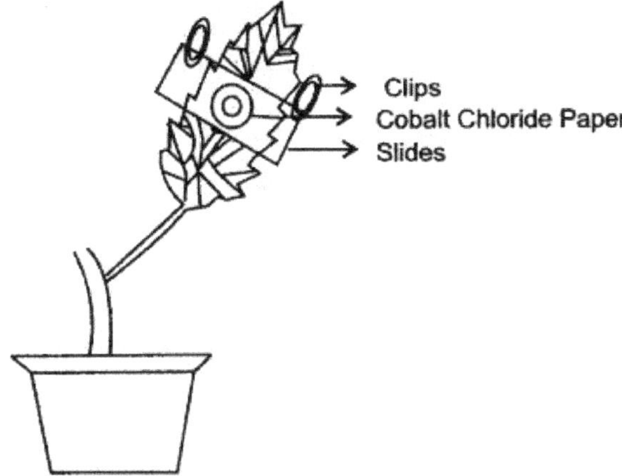

(i) What is the aim of the experiment?

(a) To prove that more transpiration occurs from the lower surface of a dicot leaf

(b) To prove that more transpiration occurs from the upper surface of a dicot leaf

(c) To prove that transpiration is equal on both sides of the leaf

(d) To prove that transpiration does not take place in a dicot leaf

Answer: (a)

(ii) What is the colour of dry Cobalt Chloride paper?

(a) Pink

(b) Blue

(c) Brown

(d) White

Answer: (b)

(iii) After about an hour, what change, if any, would you expect to find in the cobalt chloride paper placed on the upper and lower surface of the leaf?

(a) Upper Surface – Pink, Lower Surface – Blue

(b) Upper Surface – White, Lower Surface – Blue

(c) Upper Surface – less Pink, Lower Surface – more Pink

(d) Upper Surface – more Pink, Lower Surface – less Pink

Answer: (c)

(iv) Two adaptation in plants to reduce transpiration are: ______________________

(a) Narrow Leaves, Thin cuticles

(b) Fewer Stomata, Broad lamina of leaves
(c) Thin cuticles, Sunken stomata
(d) Narrow leaves, Fewer stomata
Answer: (d)

(v) The rate of transpiration is less when there is:
(a) High humidity in the air and low temperature
(b) Less humidity in the air and decrease in atmospheric pressure
(c) Bright sunlight and high temperature
(d) More wind and low intensity of sunlight
Answer: (a)

ICSE 2023 EXAMINATION

PREVIOUS YEAR PAPER-**2022**

BIOLOGY

(SCIENCE PAPER-2)

Maximum Marks: 80

Time allowed: Two hours

Answers to this Paper must be written on the paper provided separately.

You will not be allowed to write during first 15 minutes.

This time is to be spent in reading the question paper.

The time given at the head of this Paper is the time allowed for writing the answers.

(Section A is compulsory. Attempt any four questions from Section B.

The intended marks for questions or parts of questions are given in brackets [].

Section A

Answer all the questions from this section

Question 1. **[10]**

Choose the correct Answers to the questions from the given options. (Do not copy the question. Write the correct Answer: only.)

(i) The mineral element in hemoglobin:

(a) Manganese

(b) Iron

(c) Sodium

(d) Calcium

Answer: (b)

(ii) The number of cranial nerves in humans are:

(a) 12

(b) 31 pairs

(c) 31

(d) 12 pairs

Answer: (d)

(iii) Gigantism and Acromegaly are due to:

(a) Hypersecretion of Growth hormone

(b) Hyposecretion of Growth hormone

(c) Hypersecretion of Thyroxine

(d) Hyposecretion of Thyroxine

Answer: (a)

(iv) Pericardium covers the:

(a) Heart

(b) Brain

(c) Pinal cord
(d) Eyeball
Answer: (a)

(v) The circular opening in the centre of iris:
(a) Lens
(b) Cornea
(c) Sclera
(d) Pupil
Answer: (d)

(vi) The blood vessel that carries oxygenated blood is:
(a) Pulmonary artery
(b) Pulmonary vein
(c) Renal vein
(d) Hepatic vein
Answer: (b)

(vii) Organ of corti is present inside the:
(a) Cochlea
(b) Semicircular canals
(c) Sacculus
(d) Utriculus
Answer: (a)

(viii) The structure that stores urine temporarily is:
(a) Ureter
(b) Urinary bladder
(c) Urethra
(d) Kidneys
Answer: (c)

(ix) Islets of Langerhans are located in:
(a) Liver
(b) Pituitary gland
(c) Spleen
(d) Pancreas
Answer: (d)

(x) The main nitrogenous waste formed in the human body:
(a) Uric acid
(b) Ammonia

(c) Urea

(d) Creatinine

Answer: (b)

Section B

(Attempt any three questions from this Section)

Question 2.

(i) Simple goitre is usually seen in people living in the hilly regions. Give two reasons for the statement. **[2]**

(ii) What are the two types of blood circulation in humans? **[2]**

(iii) Mention the three major steps involved in the production of urine. **[3]**

(iv) Draw a neat diagram of a Neuron and label any two parts. **[3]**

Answer:

(i) Simple goiter is usually seen in people living in the hilly regions because:

(a) Iodine is deficient in the soil of hilly regions, hence in the food grown. So, people consume less iodine.

(b) Iodine is needed for the production of thyroxine. So, people suffer from simple goitre, i.e., swelling in the neck due to the deficiency of iodine.

(ii) **(a) Pulmonary Circulation:** The circulation which pertains to the lungs is called pulmonary circulation. Pulmonary artery arises from the right ventricle and carries deoxygenated blood for oxygenation to the lungs. The pulmonary vein then carries oxygenated blood from the lungs to the left atrium of the heart.

(b) Systemic Circulation: The circulation which pertains to the general body circulation is called systemic circulation. Aorta from the left ventricle carries oxygenated blood to different tissues of the body. From different tissues, the veins carry deoxygenated blood and transfer it to the right atrium via vena cava.

(iii) The urine is formed by three main steps:

(a) Filtration: The process by which the liquid part of the blood, filter out of the glomerulus into the Bowman's capsule, because of the pressure set up in the glomerulus due to the differences in diameter of the afferent and efferent arteriole.

(b) Reabsorption: The process of absorbing substances like glucose, some salts, etc. from the glomerular filtrate by the blood to the extent that the normal concentration of the blood is restored.

(c) Secretion: The process of adding materials like Na^+, H^+, etc. into the glomerular filtrate since it occurs in the distal convoluted tubule, it is also called tubular secretion.

(iv)

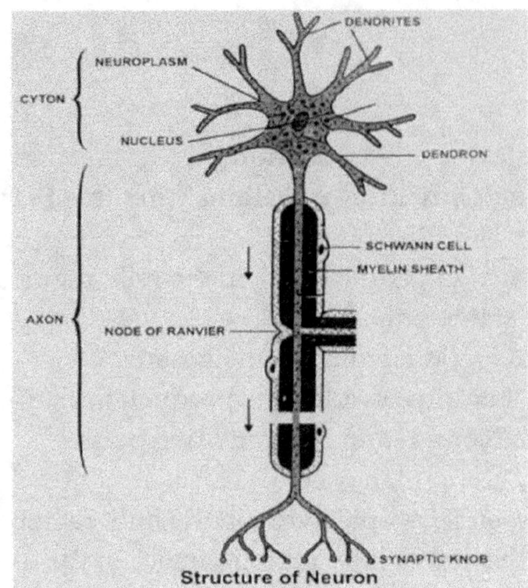

Structure of Neuron

Question 3.

(i) What is Adrenal Virilism? What causes this condition? **[2]**

(ii) Which is the light sensitive layer of the eyeball? **[2]**
Where exactly is the image formed on this layer?

(iii) Study the diagram given below and answer: the questions that follow: **[3]**

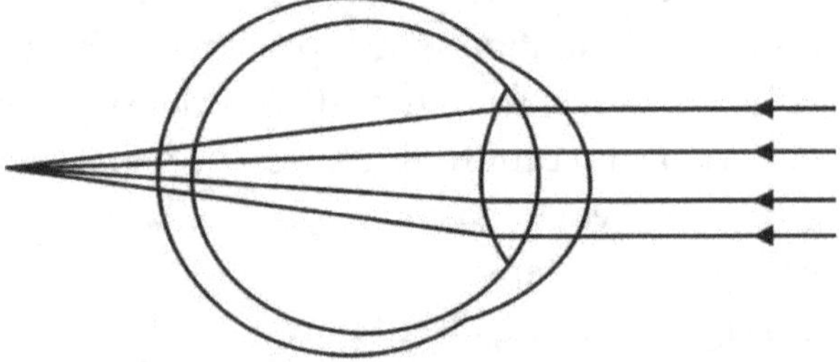

(a) Identify the defect of the eye by mentioning the technical term.

(b) Mention one reason for this defect.

(c) Name the type of lens used to correct this defect.

(iv) Give the biological terms for the three tiny bones present in the middle ear. **[3]**

Answer:

(i) When a woman develops certain male characteristics, such as beard, moustaches and deep male voice, this condition is known as adrenal virilism.
It occurs due to the overgrowth of adrenal cortex in a mature woman.

(ii) Retina is the light sensitive layer of the eyeball.
The exact image is formed on the yellow spot which is also known as Macula or Fovea centralis.

(iii) **(a)** The defect of the eye depicted is hypermetropia.
(b) Reasons for this defect are:
i. Lens is too flat.

ii. Length of eyeball becomes too short between lens and retina.

(c) A convex or converging lens.

(iv) The middle ear contains three delicate bones, called the ear ossicles. The three ear ossicles are the malleus, incus, and stapes.

Question 4.

(i) Name the endocrine gland that secretes Thyroxine. **[2]**
Give any one function of Thyroxine.

(ii) Give the full form of the abbreviation ACTH. **[2]**
Which gland secretes this hormone?

(iii) Define the term Synapse. **[3]**
How are Cytons and Axons of neurons placed in the Cerebrum?

(iv) Name the three membranous coverings of the human brain. **[3]**

Answer:

(i) Thyroid gland secretes the hormone thyroxine.

Functions of thyroxine :

i. It controls the basal metabolic rate or BMR.

ii. It regulates carbohydrate, protein and fat metabolism in the body so as to provide the best balance for growth.

iii. It maintains the body temperature.

iv. It controls muscular and nervous activity.

v. It controls mental and sexual development.

(ii) ACTH stands for Adrenocorticotropic hormone.
ACTH is secreted from the anterior lobe of pituitary gland.

(iii) The junction between the axon endings of one neuron and dendrites of the other is called synapse. In cerebrum, all the cytons of the neurons are present in the outer layers and axons are present in the inner layers.

(iv) The membranous coverings of the human brain are:

(a) Dura mater

(b) Arachnoid mater

(c) Pia mater

Question 5.

(i) Name the nerve that transmits impulses to the brain from: **[2]**

(a) Ear

(b) Eye

(ii) A mature mammalian erythrocyte lacks nucleus and mitochondria but is efficient in its functioning. Explain by giving suitable reasons. **[2]**

(iii) The diagram given below is that of a human brain. Answer: the questions that follow:

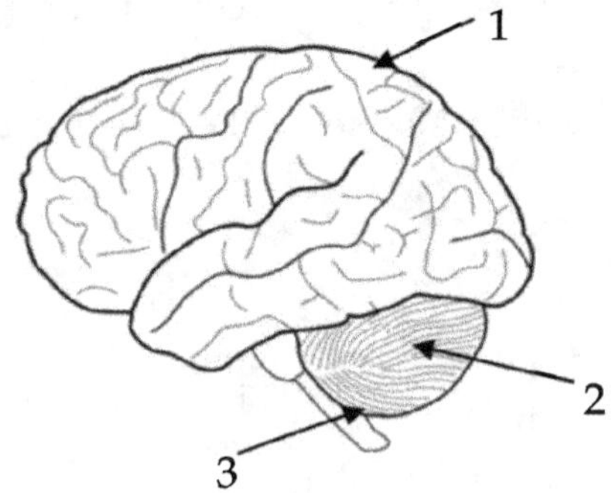

(a) Label the parts numbered 2 and 3.

(b) State any one function of the part numbered 1.

(iv) What is a reflex action? Name the two types of reflexes.

Answer:

(i) **(a)** The nerve that transmits impulses from ear to the brain is auditory nerve.

(b) The nerve that transmits impulses from eye to the brain is optic nerve.

(ii) A mature erythrocyte lacks nucleus and mitochondria because lack of nucleus enables the erythrocyte to increase the surface area-volume ratio for absorbing more oxygen and absence of mitochondria enables the erythrocyte to transport whole oxygen to the tissues without consuming oxygen hence, absence of nucleus and mitochondria does not affect the functioning of erythrocyte.

(iii) **(a)** The parts numbered 2 and 3 are as follows:

2-Cerebellum

3-Medulla oblongata

(b) The part numbered as 1 is cerebrum which is the site of intelligence, memory, thinking, thought, reason, planning and all the other voluntary actions.

(iv) Reflex action is the automatic/quick/immediate, involuntary action in body brought about by a stimulus.

The two types of reflexes are:

(a) Conditioned reflexes

(b) Unconditioned reflexes

Question 6.

(i) Give the exact location of Pulmonary semilunar valve. When does it close?

(ii) Name the hormones whose deficiency causes:

(a) Diabetes mellitus

(b) Diabetes insipidus

(iii) Draw a neat diagram of a longitudinal section of a human kidney and label Renal Cortex and Renal Medulla on the diagram.

(iv) Mention one function for each of the following:

(a) Lymphocytes

(b) Thrombocytes

(c) Neutrophils

Answer:

(i) Pulmonary semilunar valve is present between the right ventricle and the pulmonary artery.

It closes after the blood flows from right ventricle into the pulmonary artery.

(ii) **(a)** Insulin

(b) Vasopressin or antidiuretic hormone (ADH)

(iii)

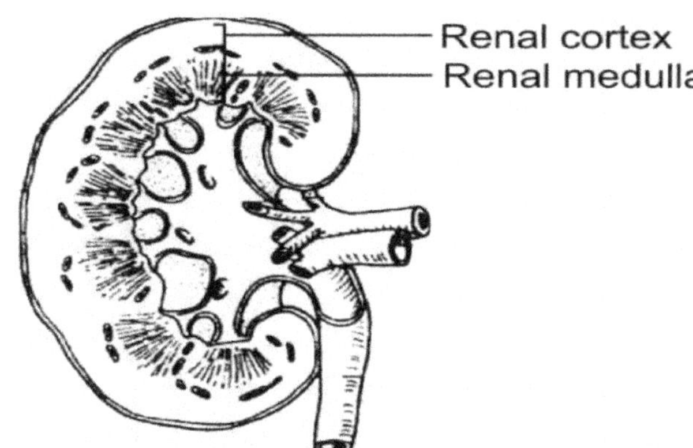

(iv) **(a) Lymphocytes:** They are the leucocytes that provide immunity by producing antibodies.

(b) Thrombocytes: They plug the blood leakage and help in clotting of blood at the site of injury.

(c) Neutrophils: They are the leucocytes that provide immunity by engulfing bacteria through the process of phagocytosis.

MOST EXPECTED QUESTION PAPER

ICSE 2023 EXAMINATION

SAMPLE TEST PAPER-1

BIOLOGY

(SCIENCE PAPER-2)

Maximum Marks: 80

Time allowed: Two hours

Answers to this Paper must be written on the paper provided separately.

You will not be allowed to write during first 15 minutes.

This time is to be spent in reading the question paper.

The time given at the head of this Paper is the time allowed for writing the answers.

(Section A is compulsory. Attempt any four questions from Section B.
The intended marks for questions or parts of questions are given in brackets [ ].

Section A

Answer all the questions from this section

Question 1. **[15]**

(i) Which of the following is a reductional division?

(a) Meiosis I.

(b) Meiosis II.

(c) Mitosis.

(d) Interphase.

Answer(a) Meiosis I.

(ii) Bead-like structures present on chromosomes are (a) telomeres.

(a) Chromomeres.

(b) Centromeres.

(c) Chromosome

(d) Chromatids

Answer(a) Chromomeres.

(iii) If a plant cell is kept in pure water, it means

(a) Cell sap has more solvent and less solute molecules as compared to external medium.

(b) Cell sap has less solvent and more solute molecules as compared to external medium.

(c) Cell sap has more solvent and more solute molecules as compared to external medium.

(d) Cell sap has less solvent and less solute molecules as compared to external medium.

Answer(a) Cell sap has more solvent and less solute molecules as compared to external medium.

(iv) Root pressure develops when

(a) Transpiration is lower than the absorption of water.

(b) Transpiration is higher than the absorption of water.

(c) Transpiration is same as the absorption of water.

(d) There is no absorption of water.
Answer(b) Transpiration is higher than the absorption of water.

(v) Transpiration pull will be maximum under which of the following conditions:
(a) Open stomata, dry atmosphere and moist soil.
(b) Open stomata, high humidity and well-irrigated soil.
(c) Open stomata, high humidity and dry soil.
(d) Closed stomata, dry atmosphere and dry soil.
Answer(c) Open stomata, high humidity and dry soil.

(vi) A plant is kept in a dark cupboard for about 48 hours before conducting any experiment photo-synthesis to:
(a) Remove starch from the plant.
(b) Ensure that starch is not translocated from the leaves.
(c) Remove chlorophyll from the leaf of the plant.
(d) Remove starch from the experimental leaf.
Answer(d) Remove starch from the experimental leaf.

(vii) The white blood cells responsible for phagocytosis of foreign organisms are
(a) Neutrophils and eosinophils.
(b) Neutrophils and basophils.
(c) Eosinophils and basophils.
(d) Lymphocytes and monocytes.
Answer(b) Neutrophils and basophils.

(viii) The presence of bile pigments in urine may indicate the presence of
(a) Glucose.
(b) Diabetes mellitus.
(c) Bacterial infection.
(d) Liver cirrhosis.
Answer(d) Liver cirrhosis.

(ix) The cerebral hemispheres in mammals are connected by
(a) Neurilemma.
(b) Corpus luteum.
(c) Pons varolii.
(d) Corpus callosum.
Answer(d) Corpus callosum.

(x) Which of the following is not a natural reflex action?
(a) Knee-jerk
(b) Salivation at the sight of food

(c) Blinking of eyes due to strong light
(d) Sneezing when any irritant enters the nose
Answer(c) Blinking of eyes due to strong light

(xi) The gland composed of both endocrine and exocrine tissues is
(a) Pituitary.
(b) Pancreas.
(c) Thyroid.
(d) Adrenal.
Answer(b) Pancreas.

(xii) The middle piece of spermatozoa provides
(a) Nutrition.
(b) Energy.
(c) Motility.
(d) Penetrating power.
Answer(b) Energy.

(xiii) The ventral root ganglion of the spinal cord contains cell bodies of the
(a) Motor neuron.
(b) Sensory neuron.
(c) Intermediate neuron.
(d) Association neuron.
Answer(d) Association neuron.

(xiv) Genes are located on the
(a) Nucleolus
(b) Ribosomes.
(c) Nuclear membrane.
(d) Chromosomes.
Answer(d) Chromosomes.

(xv) The cells of root hair have
(a) Semipermeable cell wall and permeable cell membrane.
(b) Permeable cell wall and semipermeable cell membrane.
(c) Both cell wall and cell membrane permeable.
(d) Both cell wall and cell membrane semipermeable.
Answer(b) Permeable cell wall and semipermeable cell membrane.

Question 2.

(i) Name the following: **[5]**

(a) Name a solution whose concentration is greater than that of the cell sap.

(b) Plasma protein that provides immunity.

(c) Name the valves present in human heart.

(d) An example of non-biodegradable waste.

(e) The genetic make up of an organism.

Answer

(a) Hypertonic

(b) Albunim and glabuliu

(c) Tricuspid and bicuspid

(d) Polyethene

(e) Genotype

(ii) Arrange and rewrite the terms in each group in the correct order so as to be in a logical sequence beginning with the term that is underlined. **[5]**

(a) Prophase, anaphase, metaphase, telophase

(b) Interphase, metaphase, prophase, telophase, anaphase.

(c) Karyokinessis, s-phase, cytokinesis, g_1 phase, g_2 phase

(d) Cell wall, root hair, cell membrone, cortex

(e) Absorption of light, breaking of h2o, phosphorylation, 0_2 release

Answer

(a) 1,3,2,4

(b) 1,3,2,5,4

(c) 4,2,5,3,1

(d) 2,1,3,4

(e) 1,2,3,4

(iii) Match the items given in Column I with the most appropriate ones in Column II and rewrite the correct matching pairs. **[5]**

Column I	Column II
(a) Starch test	i Grana
(b) Plasmolysis	ii Iodine solution
(c) Photolysis	iii Eosin solution
(d) Synapsis	iv Oxygenated blood
(e) Left atrium	v Pairing of homologous Chromosome
	vi Shrinkage of protoplasm
	vii Photo Oxidation of Water

Answer

(a) ii

(b) vi

(c) vii

(d) v

(e) iv

(iv) Choose the odd one out from the following terms and name the category to which the others belong: **[5]**

(a) The thyroid gland, Lacrimal gland, Pituitary gland, and Adrenal gland.

(b) Detergents, Sewage, X-rays, Oil spills

(c) The spinal cord, Cerebrum, Pons, Cerebellum

(d) Chloroplast, Cell wall, Large Vacuoles, Centrosome.

(e) Auxin, Oxytocin, Gibberellin, Cytokinin

Answer:

(a) Lacrimal gland - Endocrine Gland

(b) X-rays - Water Pollution

(c) Spinal cord - Borin

(d) Centrosome - Plant Cell

(e) Oxytocin - Plant Hormones

(v) State the exact location of the following structures: **[5]**

(a) Chiasmata

(b) Interneuron

(c) Pons

(d) SA node

(e) Sertoli cell

Answer

(a) In between homologous

(b) In the cns chromostone

(c) Bottom your skull

(d) Right upper chamber of the heart

(e) In the semintrous tubull

Section B

(Attempt any four questions from this Section.)

Question 3.

(i) Define -thyroxin **[1]**

(ii) Give one difference between phototropism and geotropism. **[2]**

(iii) What is osmosis? How many type of it. **[2]**

(iv) State the function of ethylene. **[2]**

(v) The diagram below represents a certain stage of mitosis: **[3]**

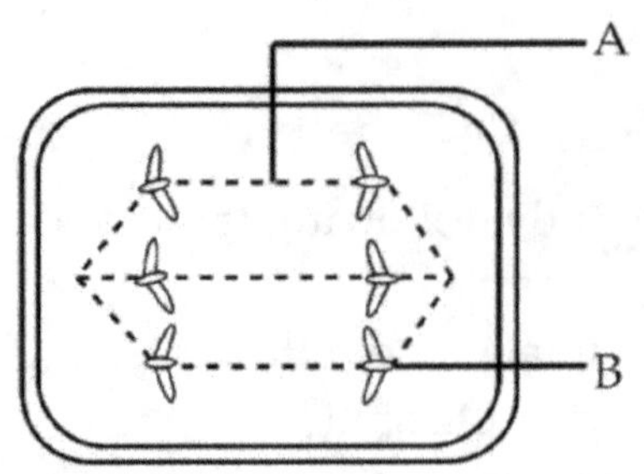

(a) Identify the stage of cell division.

(b) Name the parts labelled *A* and *B*.

(c) What is the unique feature observed in this stage?

(d) How many daughter cells are formed from this type of cell division?

Question 4.

(i) Expand the abbreviation SA node **[1]**

(ii) Name any two tropic movements. **[2]**

(iii) Shoot of the plant bends towards the light.explain by giving suitable reasons. **[2]**

(iv) Mention two pathways of blood which circulated by heart. **[2]**

(v) The given diagram represents a nephron and its blood supply. Study the diagram and answer the following questions: **[3]**

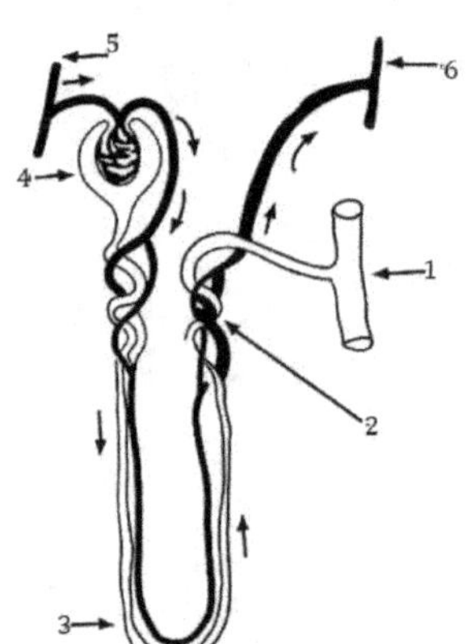

(a) Label parts 1, 2, 3 and 4.

(b) State the reason for the high hydrostatic pressure in the glomerulus.

(c) Name the blood vessel which contains the least amount of urea in this diagram.

(d) Name the two main stages of urine formation.

(e) Name the part of the nephron which lies in the renal medulla.

Question 5.

(i) Define-pulmonary semilunar valve **[1]**

(ii) Explain the function of CO_2 during photosynthesis **[2]**

(iii) What is the significance of Calvin cycle in plant? **[2]**

(iv) What is abscisic acid? Explain its role in plant. **[2]**

(v) Give the schematic representation of cell cycle. **[3]**

Question 6.

(i) Define -m phase

(ii) Differentiate between lubb and dubb.

(iii) State the function of hypothalamus with a suitable example.

(iv) The two strands of dna are exactly the same as the original one. Explain

(v) Given below is a diagrammatic representation of a defect of the human eye:

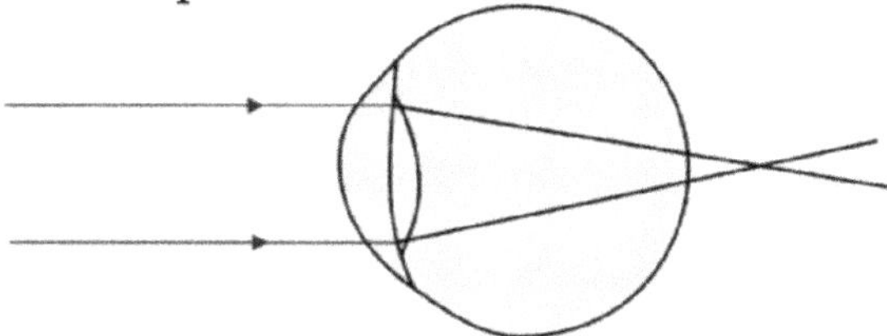

(a) Identify the defect. State how the defect can be rectified.

(b) Mention two reasons for the above defect.

(c) Name the part of the eye responsible for maintaining the shape of the eyeball.

(d) What is persistence of vision?

(e) Define the terms 'accommodation' and 'normal vision' in relation to eye.

Question 7.

(i) Explain- recombination

(ii) Give reason why mendal choose pea plant for his experiment.

(iii) Mention two functions of antibody which present on the surface of rbc.

(iv) What is the difference between grey matter and white matter.

(v) Draw a neat labelled generalized structure of a neuron.

Question 8.

(i) Define- fallopian tube

(ii) Potato slice in salt solution exhibit flaccid but in plain water become crisp. Why?

(iii) Differentiate between renal artery and renal vein.

(iv) State two disadvantages of transpiration.

(v) The diagram given alongside represents a cross section of the human eye.

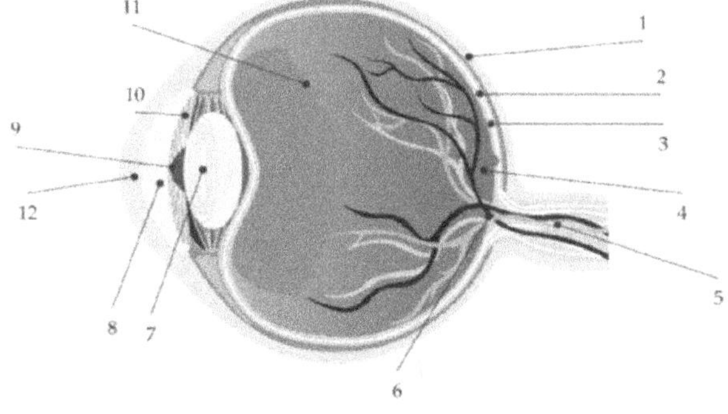

(a) Name the parts labelled 1 to 12.

(b) Give the function of parts labelled 7 and 9.

(c) Give the function of the parts labelled 3 and 4.

(d) Why is the part labelled 6 called the blind spot?

(e) What would happen if the part labelled 5 is damaged?

The diagram given alongside represents the external view of the human brain. Study

ICSE 2023 EXAMINATION

SAMPLE TEST PAPER-2

BIOLOGY

(SCIENCE PAPER-2)

Maximum Marks: 80

Time allowed: Two hours

Answers to this Paper must be written on the paper provided separately.

You will not be allowed to write during first 15 minutes.

This time is to be spent in reading the question paper.

The time given at the head of this Paper is the time allowed for writing the answers.

(Section A is compulsory. Attempt any four questions from Section B.

The intended marks for questions or parts of questions are given in brackets [ ].

Section A

Answer all the questions from this section

Question 1. **[15]**

(i) The term mitosis was coined by

(a) Flemming.

(b) Watson.

(c) Strasburger

(d) Virchow.

Answer(a) Flemming.

(ii) A plant cell may burst when

(a) Cell wall on the plasma membrane

(b) Turgor pressure exceeds wall pressure

(c) Wall pressure exceeds turgor pressure.

(d) Cell loses turgidity.

Answer(b) Turgor pressure exceeds wall pressure

(iii) Water moves from the cortex of the root to

(a) Endodermis.

(b) Root hair.

(c) Pericycle.

(d) Xylem tissue.

Answer(a) Endodermis

(iv) The protein responsible for maintaining the osmotic pressure of blood is

(a) Globulin.

(b) Albumin.

(c) Fibrin.

(d) Fibrinogen.

Answer(b) Albumin.

(v) Which of the following cell organelles form more than half of the membranous content of the cell?
(a) ER
(b) Mitochondria
(c) Golgi complex
(d) Ribosomes
Answer(a) ER

(vi) Which is the most appropriate stage to count the number of chromosomes?
(a) Prophase
(b) Interphase
(c) Metaphase
(d) Telophase
Answer(c) Metaphase

(vii) Identify the reaction that does not occur during the light phase.
(a) Absorption of light by chlorophyll
(b) Photolysis of water
(c) Reduction of NADP
(d) Formation of sugar
Answer(d) Formation of sugar

(viii) Which region of the kidney is composed of cone-shaped structures called renal pyramids?
(a) Cortex
(b) Bowman's capsule
(c) Medulla
(d) Renal pelvis
Answer(c) Medulla

(ix) Which component present in the blood helps in the transport of oxygen as well as carbon dioxide?
(a) Hemoglobin
(b) Plasma
(c) Cytoplasm
(d) Heparin
Answer(a) Hemoglobin

(x) Which part of the sperm duct is used for storing the sperm temporarily?
(a) Rete testis
(b) Vasa efferentia
(c) Epididymis
(d) Vasa deferentia

Answer(c) Epididymis

(xi) Identify the cells that provide nutrition to the germ cells.
(a) Sertoli cells
(b) Leydig cells
(c) Seminiferous
(d) Septa
Answer(a) Sertoli cells

(xii) Which nerves transmit the electrical impulses from the central nervous system to the muscles and glands?
(a) Sensory neurons
(b) Motor neurons
(c) Mixed neurons
(d) Peripheral neurons
Answer(a) Sensory neurons

(xiii) Which phytohormone inhibits the growth of the plant?
(a) Auxins
(b) Cytokinins
(c) Abscisic acid
(d) Gibberellins
Answer(c) Abscisic acid

(xiv) Which among the following phytohormone is involved in the growth of plants?
(a) Auxins
(b) Gibberellins
(c) Abscisic acid
(d) Both (a) and (b)
Answer(d) Both (a) and (b)

(xv) Unburnt carbon released during the burning of fuels is a kind of
(a) Gaseous pollutant
(b) Particulate pollutant.
(c) Radioactive pollutant.
(d) Radiation pollutant.
Answer(b) Particulate pollutant.

Question 2.

(i) Name the following: **[5]**
(a) Name the membrane that disappears during the late prophase.
(b) The phenotypic and genotypic results of dihybrid crosses.
(c) Inward movement of water molecules through a semipermeable membrane of a cell.

(d) The process of uptake of mineral ions against the concentration gradient using energy from the cell.

(e) Last part of the nephron carries urine to the ureters.

(ii) Arrange and rewrite the terms in each group in the correct order so as to be in a logical sequence beginning with the term that is underlined. **[5]**

(a) Implantation, Ovulation, Parturition Fertilisation, Gestation.

(b) Intestine, Hepatic Portal Vein, Hepatic Vein.Intestinal artery, Liver

(c) Sensory neuron, Spinal cord, Motor neuron, Effector, Receptor.

(d) Conjunctiva cornea, pupil, lens, yellow spot, blind spot.

(e) Pinna ,auditory canal ,ear ossicles, cochlea, tympanum.

(iii) Match the items given in Column I with the most appropriate ones in Column II and rewrite the correct matching pairs. **[5]**

Colum 1	Column I
1. Neutrophils	Gonad
2. Testis	Iron
3. Clotting of blood	Calcium
4. Transpiration	prostate gland
5. Uriniferous tubule	Water vapour
	Water droplest
	Uterus
	Protection

(iv) Choose the odd one out from the following terms and name the category to which the others belong: **[5]**

(a) Menopause, ovulation,Follicle,semen,menarche.

(b) Nerve, Reflex, Effectors, Gonad, stimulus.

(c) Diapedesis, Plasma, WBC, demography, RBC

(d) Cuticular, photometer, plasmolysis, Guttation

(e) Nucleosome, Chromosome, Microsome, centrosome, centrioles.

(v) State the exact location of the following structures: **[5]**

(a) Furrow

(b) Yellow spot

(c) Sperm duct

(d) Beta cells

(e) Eardrum

Section B

(Attempt any four questions from this Section.)

Question 3.

(i) Define-Beses in DNA **[1]**

(ii) Give the difference between DNA and Histone **[2]**

(iii) What is Carrier? Give one example. **[2]**

(iv) State that the Conduction of nerve impulse through a nerve fibre. **[2]**

(v) The diagram given below represents a defect of vision of the human eye. **[3]**

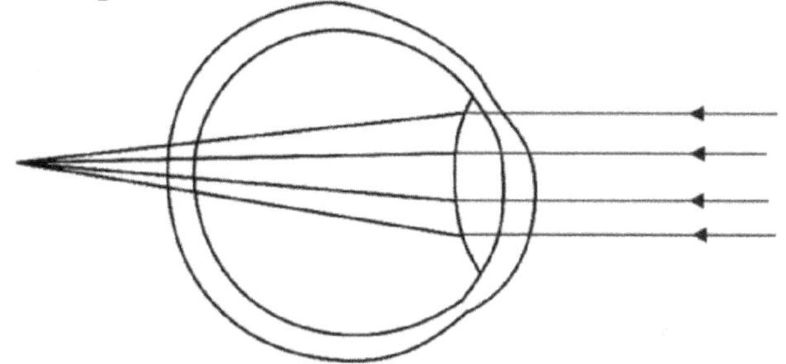

(a) Name the defect.

(b) What is the effect of this defect on man?

(c) Mention two causes for this defect.

(d) How can this defect be rectified?

Question 4.

(i) Expand the abbreviation - CNS **[1]**

(ii) Name any two nerves. **[2]**

(iii) Hypertonic solution of salt can inhibit the growth of the plant and further palnt leads to die. Explain it with suitable reasons. **[2]**

(iv) Mention two adaptations in a plant to reduce excessive transpiration. **[2]**

(v) Look at the figures A, B and C carefully and answer the questions which follow: **[3]**

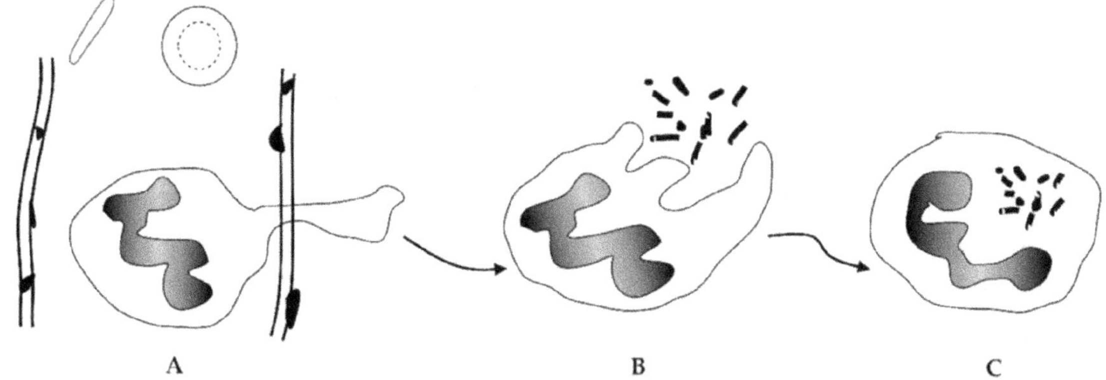

(a) Which kind of blood vessel is shown in A? Write any two characteristics of such blood vessels.

(b) Name the two kinds of blood cells shown in A.

(c) Describe step by step what is happening in the three figures. What is the advantage of this activity to our body?

Question 5.

(i) Define-Evaporation **[1]**

(ii) What is the significance of sunken stomata? **[2]**

(iii) State two functions of the internal ear. **[2]**

(iv) What is the dominant trait in mendelian genetics how it helps in variation? **[2]**

(v) Draw a neat, labeled diagram of double circulation in the heart and hepatic portal system through the liver. **[3]**

Question 6.

(i) Define-Blood pressure **[1]**

(ii) Differentiate between Homozygous dominant and Homozygous recessive. **[2]**

(iii) State the function of Ganong's potometer with a suitable example. **[2]**

(iv) Baldness is generally seen in males. Explain **[2]**

(v) Given alongside is the diagram of an apparatus set up to study a very important physiological process. **[3]**

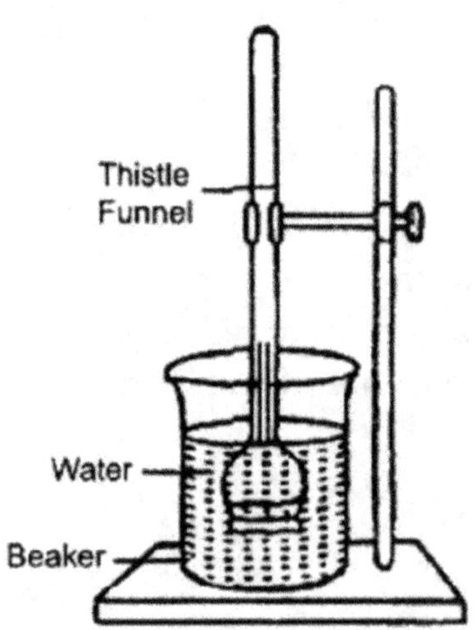

(a) Name the process being studied.

(b) Explain the process.

(c) What change would you observe in the thistle funnel containing sugar solution after about 10 minutes?

(d) Is sugar solution hypertonic or hypotonic?

(e) Name the part of the plant cell which is represented by the sugar solution.

Question 7.

(i) Explain-Vehicular air pollution **[1]**

(ii) Give the reasons why Chromosomes are highly condensed. **[2]**

(iii) Mention two functions of Rods. **[2]**

(iv) What is the difference between light-dependent and light-independent reactions. **[2]**

(v) Draw a neat, labeled diagram of the accommodation of the eye for a distant and near object. **[3]**

Question 8.

(i) Define-Myopia. **[1]**

(ii) Defect in which some parts of the object are seen in focus while others are blurred. Explain. **[2]**

(iii) Differentiate between the left and right chambers of the heart. **[2]**

(iv) Given below is the figure of the root. **[2]**

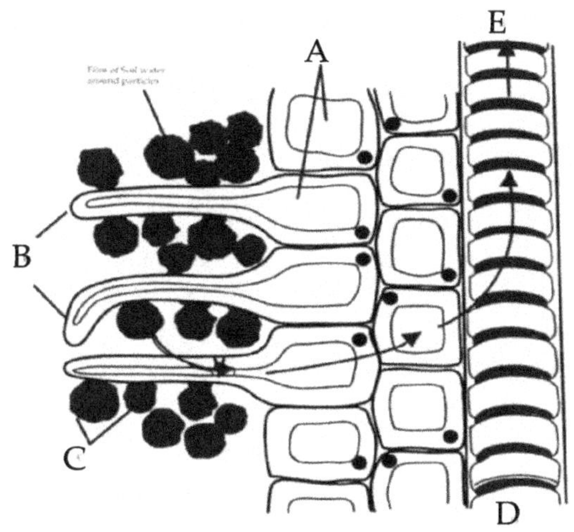

(a) What does this figure depict?

(b) What do the arrows in the figure show?

(c) Label the parts A to E.

www.ingramcontent.com/pod-product-compliance
Lightning Source LLC
LaVergne TN
LVHW080607200726
843509LV00007B/260

* 9 7 8 9 3 5 5 5 6 4 9 1 7 *